THE IDEAL OF THE UNIVERSITY

The Ideal
of the University

by Robert Paul Wolff

BEACON PRESS BOSTON

For Tobias Barrington, on
further reflection

First published by Beacon Press in 1969
First published as a Beacon Paperback in 1970

International Standard Book Number: 0–8070–3189–5

Beacon Press books are published under the auspices
of the Unitarian Universalist Association
Published simultaneously in Canada by Saunders of Toronto, Ltd.
Printed in the United States of America

Contents

Preface

This book is both the expression of a lifelong concern for the principles and purposes of higher education and a response to events at Columbia which, at this writing, are barely twelve months past. Reflections on the nature of teaching and learning have been a part of the philosophic enterprise at least since the time of Socrates, so it is entirely proper that philosophers today should resist the tendency of sociologists, psychologists, and professors of education to appropriate the subject for themselves.

My attitudes toward matters of educational philosophy and policy can be traced to three quite disparate sources. First in time and in importance was the impact on me of a number of great teachers with whom I studied as an undergraduate at Harvard. From Harry Austyn Wolfson, Willard Van Orman Quine, and Clarence Irving Lewis I learned what scholarship, clarity, precision, and philosophical commitment could be. In the years since, I have met and taught with men whose lives and work embody those same values—Barrington Moore, Jr., Hans Morgenthau, Herbert Marcuse, and many others. My admiration for these men in a sense sets limits to my speculation about educational reform, for no ideal of the university could possibly win my allegiance unless it made room for them to pursue their work with freedom and with honor.

A second influence, particularly on my thinking about institutional reform, has been the writings of Paul Goodman and a small number of other iconoclastic social critics of a similar style. From time to time a man comes along with the knack of seeing things in an entirely different way, as though he were able to get a look at them from a perspective denied the rest of us. Goodman seems to me to possess something of that capacity. I do not always agree with him about educational matters, but I always put down one of his books or essays with the dismaying feeling that until that moment I have not really understood the subject at all.

The third and most recent influence on the views in this book is my encounter with the three score Columbia and Barnard undergraduates who took my course on social philosophy in the Fall of 1968. I chose to devote the semester to a discussion of the university in American life, and as a consequence many of the most active and concerned undergraduates on the Morningside Heights campus elected to take the course. Their arguments, objections, and suggestions have done much to dislodge me from the rather crusty traditionalism to which I was initially committed. Had I written this book before confronting them, I think I would have taken a very different position on grading and on the role of students in the making of major university decisions. Since my classroom manner is hardly timid or diffident, they may not have realized the extent of their impact on me. This Preface may perhaps serve to assure them that they got through to me.

The present work began as a series of lectures supported by the Matchette Foundation and delivered at the University of Wisconsin in Madison on April 14, 16, and 17, 1969. I am grateful to the Foundation for making the lectures possible, and to the Department of Philosophy for the invitation which spurred me to set down my thoughts on paper. The warmth of their hospitality encourages me to hope that the students and faculty in Madison will find this work to their liking.

New York City
May 1969

Introduction

These reflections on the ideal of a university have their immediate origin in the much-publicized student uprising on the campus of Columbia University during the Spring of 1968. When the first group of militant students seized Hamilton Hall, I was preparing to leave for a brief speaking trip in the Midwest. As revolutionary communes were set up in the Administration building and several classroom buildings, I was lecturing at the University of Wisconsin on the "concept of political community." Rushing back from my lecture to see the real thing in the making, I became embroiled in the endless activities of debate, negotiation, and attempted accommodation which were punctuated, but not ended, by the two late-night police raids. Though much less actively involved in the affair than many of my colleagues, some of whom virtually lived on the campus for weeks on end, I devoted more waking hours to the principles, organization, and rationale of a modern university than I would ever have thought the subject could sustain.

During the playing out of the events themselves, as well as in the months of retrospection which followed, my principal emotion was neither elation nor despair, but rather an irritated uneasiness at my inability to determine where my sympathies in the affair should lie. Almost immediately, the participants were tagged with the familiar labels of the left-right political spectrum. Apologists for the Administration, of whom there were very few, were universally labeled right-wing, despite the fact that their number included several well-known liberals. Those who supported the Students for a Democratic Society (SDS) in all its demands were naturally considered far left, and everyone else was positioned somewhere in between. As a self-proclaimed radical, it seemed natural that I should gravitate leftward, stopping short perhaps of the fringe inhabited by what one relatively sober SDS member called "action freaks." But the more deeply I became involved in the affair, the less satisfied I was with the conventional labels and their political implications. There was no position along that one-dimensional distribution of opinions that I could comfortably claim as mine.

At first, I supposed the problem to lie within me—an ambivalence, perhaps, between my sympathy for protest and my identification with the authority represented by the faculty. But as I sought to arrange my thoughts, I began to realize that the confusion lay not in my sentiments but in my concepts. Before I could decide where I stood on such issues as student power, participatory democracy, value neutrality, and educational relevance, I needed a much more coherent theory of what a university is, and what a university ought to be. In a war, one can rely upon the maxim, "The enemy of my enemy is my friend." But when a social institution like a university is in the process of being reconstructed, it is not so easy to tell friends from enemies.

As I brooded on these matters, I received an invitation from the University of Wisconsin to deliver the Matchette Lectures there in the Spring of 1969. I grasped the opportunity to put my thoughts in order and lay them before a university community from which I could hope for a sympathetic but critical response. This book, in turn, is an outgrowth of those lectures. It is a deliberate attempt to combine very general reflections on the nature of a university with some particular observations about universities and university education in the United States at the present time. As these prefatory remarks indicate, the philosophy of education set forth here is more than ordinarily motivated by practical concerns. I am, to be sure, in pursuit of the universal form or Idea of the university, as Plato would put it; but my aim is not so to enrapture myself with that pure form that I forget the pale embodiments of it which provoked my search. Rather, my purpose is to develop a program of practical reform of present-day institutions of higher education in America, and only incidentally to sketch the ground plan for a utopian university in the ideal society for which I yearn.

One word of clarification before we begin. This book presents itself as dealing with the ideal of the *university*. But in the United States, for a variety of historical reasons which are accidental and peculiar to the American experience, virtually every university is organized around an undergraduate college. In some cases, as in the Ivy League, the colleges long preceded the establishment of graduate and professional schools and the adoption of the title "university." In other cases, the creation of the university was virtually contemporaneous with that of the central college. There are even a few universities which instituted undergraduate programs only after they had established their graduate programs. But whatever the sequence of development, American universities are now committed to a combination of undergraduate and graduate programs.

The problems posed by this fusion are, in my opinion, a major source of the educational confusion which reigns on most university campuses in America today. I am one of those teachers who believe that the aims and principles of undergraduate education are totally distinct from those of graduate training. At virtually every stage of our discussion, therefore, I shall try to show how the conflict between the ideals of undergraduate and graduate education has undermined higher education in America.

THE IDEAL OF THE UNIVERSITY

PART ONE

Four Models of a University

In the opening pages of his famous lecture on "Politics as a Vocation," Max Weber undertakes to develop a sociological definition of the state. Setting himself against an old tradition, he specifically refuses to attempt a definition in terms of the ends or purposes of the state, for he says, "there is scarcely any task that some political association has not taken in hand, and there is no task that one could say has always been exclusive and peculiar to those associations which are designated as political ones." Instead, Weber offers a definition in terms of the *means* by which all states have pursued their ends, namely, physical force.

If we were interested here in developing a sociological definition of the university, in discovering the common and defining marks of the social institutions which actually go by the name of "university" in America today, we would be equally ill-advised to focus upon ends and purposes. Universities have been founded for all manner of reasons: to preserve an old faith, to proselytize a new one, to train skilled workers, to raise the standards of the professions, to expand the frontiers of knowledge, and even to educate the young. Were we to seize upon some one of the many purposes of American universities as *the* purpose, we would be in the uncomfortable position of appearing to claim that most of the so-called universities in the country are not "really" universities at all. There is not a great deal of illumination to be gained from such a course.

But since we are concerned with the *ideal* of the university, with the way it should be rather than with the way it is, there is for us no better course than to attend to ends and purposes. Without a coherent notion of what a university is for—some idea of what it should be and do—we cannot possibly evaluate existing universities; nor can we make rational proposals for university reform unless we have already decided on the direction in which we think the institution ought to move.

Confronted with a task so obviously value laden, some students of American education will want to shrink into a more "objective" study, such as an investigation of the educational ideals which the founders and governors of universities have themselves actually cherished. There is much to be said for such a study, but it won't solve our problem, for even after we know what American educators have sought to accomplish in their universities, we must still decide whether they were *right*. In the end, empirical data about the character and direction of American universities, as well as information about the guiding ideals of their administrators, will be less important to us than the philosophical arguments which can be advanced in support of those ideals.

I shall begin our investigation by sketching four models of a university. Each model is a picture of an imaginary university which embodies one particular set of ideals and is organized on an appropriate principle of internal authority. Needless to say, these models are not intended to be representations of actual institutions. Indeed, they are not even really intended as accounts of possible institutions. Rather, they are what Weber called "ideal types"—thought-experiments by means of which we can trace out some of the connections between a particular conception of university education and the institutional arrangements, social conditions, entrance requirements, and purposes which naturally follow from it.

Several of these models have long lived in the minds of university teachers and administrators, and they have thus been partial causes of the universities which now flourish in America. Other models are urged upon us by partisans of university reform, and hence they play a role in current debates. My purpose in beginning with a series of abstract models is threefold: First, as I have indicated, I wish to trace out the connections between the ideals themselves and the institutional arrangements which might embody them. Secondly, I want to clarify somewhat the confused reality of university education by showing how conflicting ideals have become intertwined in strange institutional combinations.

For example, the practice of beginning a college education with one or two years of general education, and completing it with the writing of a very professional-looking honors thesis, makes no sense at all until we see that it grows out of a compromise between two antithetical ideals of undergraduate education. Finally, and most important, I want to confront the various ideals as ideals, and try to decide which of them really *should* dominate American higher education. In thus making the normative question central, I reflect the domination of practical over theoretical concerns in my own mind.

   The four models to be discussed are:

   The University as a Sanctuary of Scholarship
   The University as a Training Camp for the Professions
   The University as a Social Service Station
   The University as an Assembly Line for Establishment Man

   The first model is drawn from the history of the university; the second model reflects its present character; the third is a projection of present trends and thus is a prediction of the shape of the university to come; and the fourth is a radical critique of the university, an anti-model, as it were. None of them, I might say, perfectly embodies my ideals and preferences. That must wait for Part Three and the Conclusion.

CHAPTER ONE

The University as a Sanctuary of Scholarship

The most familiar image of the university is the ivory tower, symbol of the sanctuary within which the scholar quietly pursues his bookish calling. The scholar is the man of learning, the *Gelehrte*, the reader of languages ancient and modern, who laboriously masters the literature of the great humanistic tradition together with the commentaries which his predecessors have made upon it, and then carries that tradition a step forward with his own original contribution. The scholarly life is removed from the immediate affairs of the social order. Quiet, contemplative, frequently celibate, it is enlivened by bookish disputes of remarkable virulence in which a footnote can wound as deeply as a sword and a book review crush with fatal force. The truly great scholars are men of enormous stature within the world of the university. Unprepossessing though they may be in personal appearance and address, an aura surrounds them like that which descends upon the winner of a Nobel Prize. Every member of the academic world carries within himself some image of a professor who is, for him, the embodiment of the ideal of scholarship. Mine is of the great Harvard medievalist Harry Austyn Wolfson.

The activity of scholarship has its historical roots in at least three older activities, from which it derives its characteristic norms and style. Most ancient, is the study of religious texts which flourished in the Hebrew, Christian, and Islamic tradition of the ancient and medieval world. The object of study was not the world—neither of ideas nor of men—but a body of writings divinely inspired, together with the steadily accumulating commentaries of previous scholars. The intense, minute concentration upon every syllable and nuance of the text was justified by its Godly origin. No mortal product could sustain so many centuries of interpretation! Obviously, this activity of scholarly exegesis demanded a mastery of the text together with the accretion of commentary. It called for encyclopedic knowledge, precision, completeness, and a self-effacing impersonality. After all, if I make so bold as to comment upon the word of God, it is not I who should be the center of attention.

To this activity of textual commentary was added a second sort of study of texts during the Renaissance of the thirteenth, fourteenth, and fifteenth centuries. The appearance in the West of new versions of the ancient religious writings, together with a new and more critical attitude toward the received texts, stimulated a widespread attempt at the rectification of the Old and New Testaments. The Latin Vulgate of St. Jerome was seen to embody countless textual corruptions and mistranslations from the original Hebrew, Aramaic, and Greek. Implausible as the connection may seem, one can trace a line of historical ancestry from Erasmus's attempts to establish the precise wording of God's revelations to man, to the present-day attempts of the Modern Language Association to provide definitive editions of the works of American novelists.

At roughly the same time, Italian scholars, poets, and artists rediscovered the literature and art of the ancient world. The rebirth of classical culture stimulated an enormous scholarly search for Roman and Greek literature. Significantly, this body of writings was secular, not divine. It would seem natural therefore not to place such great emphasis on the correction of the text, for it could scarcely be a matter of transcendent importance if some ancient poet's words were misconstrued or even lost entirely.

Nevertheless, a devotion equal to that with which religious texts had been studied was dedicated to the literary remains of classical antiquity, with consequences which are still felt in centers of humanistic study today.

Thus the activity of scholarship is in the first instance a religious and literary activity, directed toward a given corpus of texts, either divine or secular, around which a literature of commentary has accumulated. The corpus is finite, clearly defined, growing slowly as each stage in the progress of Western civilization deposits its masterpieces in the Great Tradition. Though the tradition may contain pregnant, emotionally powerful commentaries upon life and men's affairs, the scholar's concern is with the textual world, not with the world about which the text speaks. At its best, scholarship develops a refined sensibility and a wise appreciation of the complexities and ironies of the ways of God and man; at its worst, scholarship hardens into a stultifying pedantry which lacks the wit and creative genius of those who wrote the great texts.

Scholarship, in this central role of the transmission and commentary upon a divine or secular corpus, is preeminently an activity of what today is called the Humanities. Quite obviously it is antithetical to the spirit of the theoretical or experimental sciences. A physics which confined itself to commentaries on the original texts of Ptolemy, Aristotle, and Archimedes would indeed grace the halls of scholarship, but it would hardly succeed in explaining the behavior of falling bodies, let alone making an airplane that could fly. (Indeed, in most colleges and universities today, the study of the classic texts of science is left to those students who fail to exhibit any aptitude for science itself. Imagine relegating Donne and Shakespeare to the unpoetical undergraduate!) Nor does the ideal of scholarship truly flourish in the social sciences. There have been men of great learning, such as Max Weber; but society itself, not a body of texts, is the object of the social scientist's attention.

The ideal of scholarship has spawned a curious pedagogical offspring in the undergraduate curriculum. The conception of a defined textual corpus is broadened somewhat to become the familiar image of a great cultural tradition, and the theory of General Education emerges. According to this conception, Western civilization is a millennia-long dialogue among great thinkers, whose debates over the eternal questions are embodied in a number of transcendentally great works of literature and philosophy. Rising in the ancient Mediterranean and in the Near East, the two tributaries of Judeo-Christian and Graeco-Roman thought flow into a mighty cultural river, which rolls down through the Middle Ages to modern times.

This tradition is the intellectual heritage of Western man. The fundamental purpose of a college education is to initiate the student into the dialogue, acquaint him with the great ideas in these various literary embodiments, and develop that sensitivity and responsiveness which will allow him to share the tradition with fellow initiates.

The scholars whose careful work preserves the great texts are also educated men, conversant with the major works across the entire breadth of the tradition. A university which embodies this ideal is thus a community of scholars and students who converse about a common literature. Even though the subtleties of advanced scholarship may be appreciated by only a few specialists, nevertheless every member of the community can at least serve as an informed audience for the several experts.

Once the ideal of scholarship is laid out, we can easily enough infer the institutional arrangements in which it will find its most natural embodiment. The university will be a self-governing company of scholars, joined by a number of apprentice-scholars whose studies are guided by the senior professors under whom they work. The university as a community will be small, informally organized, heavy with tradition, and governed in large measure by the commitment of its members to the life of scholarship. It will have little to do in a regular way with the larger society, keeping very much to its own affairs and judging its activities by the internal norms of scholarship rather than by social norms of productivity or usefulness.

I take it there is very little real opposition to the ideals and activity of the sort of scholarship I have been describing. Even the most enthusiastic partisans of scientific research or social service commonly pay at least passing homage to the world of genuine scholarship. Many have decried the pedantry of false scholarship, and some have fought to free the social sciences from the grip of inappropriate scholarly ideals; but, save in present-day China, where the opposition to scholarship has a special political significance, there is widespread—and, I believe, justified—agreement that humanistic scholars must retain a place in any plan for the ideal university.

There is, unfortunately, rather less agreement on the companion proposition that scholarship cannot be the *sole* occupant of the university. Even in this age of science, there are traditionalists who would drive out of the university all those who study life instead of books or substitute experiments for footnotes. My favorite example of this extraordinary narrowness of vision comes, of course, from the University of Chicago, where devotion to the great tradition, particularly as it flows from Aristotle, for a time became frozen in curricula, reading lists, and degree requirements. Some while ago, the question was raised in a meeting of the Chicago College Faculty whether history should be added to the contents of the general education program. A dedicated acolyte of the Tradition rose to argue against the proposal. In support of his position, with characteristic medieval deference to authority, he quoted the passage in the *Poetics* in which Aristotle argues that history is an inferior discipline because it deals only with particulars whereas poetry deals with universals. What is striking is not that this argument carried the day—in fact it lost, and history took its place alongside poetry and philosophy in the general education curriculum—but simply that those present considered it a perfectly respectable and relevant argument! It is roughly as though Henry Ford II were to try to dissuade Walter Reuther from demanding a pay raise by appeal to the medieval doctrine of the just wage!

Whatever else we include in our utopian model, a place must be assured to Harry Wolfson, Moses Hadas, Erich Auerbach, Paul Kristeller, and all the other great *Gelehrten.* And I for one will break a lance for the theory of the great tradition at least as *one element* in an undergraduate curriculum. We deal here in matters of intellectual taste, about which there is much disputing, but no deciding. I cannot truthfully claim that men are inevitably spiritually crippled by their unfamiliarity with the great tradition, nor is initiation into its subtleties a precondition for the creation of new works of intellect. Certainly no one of my leftish leanings would see any *political* merit in a cultural tradition which has so often served as an armory of reaction. There is much to be said for the childlike innocence of those antitraditionalists who, in Michael Oakeshott's lovely phrase, strive to live each day as though it were their first. Still, I confess that I *like* a cultivated man or woman, on whom allusion is not lost, in whose discourse there echo earlier voices, one capable of that special sort of irony which comes from the awareness that one's most precious thoughts have been anticipated.

So in *my* ideal university, though not perhaps in yours, a quiet quadrangle will be set aside for the scholar; and I shall accord him thus a deference which I would not show to merely rich or powerful men.

CHAPTER TWO

The University as a Training Camp for the Professions

A more recent conception with quite different implications for the process of education is the ideal of the university as a training camp for the professions. The universities founded in Europe in the twelfth and thirteenth centuries consisted of faculties of law, medicine, and theology; and the first two of these at least remain the leading professional faculties of the present-day university. In the American experience, it was the need for clergymen that prompted the establishment of colleges in the colonial period. Only later in the nineteenth century did institutions of higher education begin to accumulate the penumbra of professional faculties to which we now attach the distinctive title, "university."*

The ideal of the professional school presupposes the existence of a number of socially defined occupational roles or categories whose characteristics correspond roughly to what we customarily mean by a "profession."** Such occupational roles are organized as self-regulating, self-certifying groups of men and women who

---

* For a first-rate discussion of the growth and present condition of professional schools in America, see *The Academic Revolution,* by Christopher Jencks and David Riesman (New York: Doubleday, 1968), especially Chapter 5. Although my discussion here deals with somewhat different questions, I have benefited enormously from their encyclopedic knowledge and sociological analysis.

** The terms "profession" and "calling" have etymological implications which have been pretty much lost in recent years. It may be that a doctor or lawyer or college teacher *ought* to "profess" something, or ought to be "called" to his position as a minister was once said to be called by God, but if so, that is now clearly a prescription and hardly a description. It may still be the case that God calls many and chooses few, but the statistics on admissions to professional schools are not nearly so discouraging.

possess and exercise a special skill or body of technical knowledge. Characteristically, a *professional* submits his work for evaluation to other members of the profession rather than to his clients, over whom he asserts an authority born of expertise. Professions vary, of course, and a lawyer is typically less independent of his client than a doctor, more independent than an architect. Nevertheless, the essential and defining mark of the professional is his dependence upon other professionals for his certification in the profession. A businessman need not persuade other businessmen of his competence before he launches a company, nor must a steelworker pass tests set by other steelworkers. But a lawyer must be certified by lawyers, a minister by ministers, a doctor by doctors, and a teacher by teachers. Much of the high social status of the professions in American society derives from this autonomy of certification, for it is a kind of power which confers dignity on its wielders. Rich men have been known to buy mayors, governors, even United States senators, but H. L. Hunt himself could not purchase certification from Harvard Medical School or a doctorate in art history from Columbia University.

The high status (and correspondingly elevated incomes) of the professions serves as a permanent spur to professionalization of the most diverse occupational roles. To the traditional quartet of law, medicine, theology, and philosophy (in the old sense of systematic rational investigation of man and the universe—what was once called Moral Philosophy and Natural Philosophy) have been added such job categories as architecture, primary- and secondary-school teaching, urban planning, business administration, diplomacy, landscape gardening, undertaking, warfare, social work, and even the performing arts. In each case, the same moves are made: first, it is claimed that the activity rests upon a body of knowledge and technique which is capable of being formulated in principles and taught in the classroom; then, the natural conclusion is drawn that only an expert practitioner can teach the activity to others and *judge whether the student has mastered it*; from this, it follows that professional schools should be established, entrance requirements fixed, degrees granted, and state-appointed boards of certification set up so that only those qualified to practice the profession will be legally permitted to do so. In some cases, the very highest level of professionalization is achieved: the practitioners reserve to themselves the role of judging what *ends* their clients should aim at, as well as what *means* they should employ. Thus, we need expert doctors to tell us not only how to achieve the physical condition we desire, but even what physical condition we *ought* to desire. Lawyers, on the other hand, are not expected to set goals for their clients, but simply to facilitate whatever plans are already projected.

Roughly speaking, a profession comes pretty close to what Plato called a *techné* in the *Republic* and the *Gorgias*. Plato saw quite clearly that the notion of *techné*, resting as it did on an objective theory of the good for man, was deeply antidemocratic. He had contempt, as we do, for the medical quack who sought to make his patient feel good momentarily without really curing his illness; but Plato took the natural next step from which we shrink, and concluded that the rules of a state had a similar obligation to minister to the true health of the body politic, rather than merely pandering to its ignorant craving for flattery. We echo this aristocratic ideal in our use of the term "statesman" to describe the proposer of unpopular measures. In the end, however, we give our hearts to the panderers who get elected, thus proving that in America today, politics is not yet a profession.

The transformation of occupational roles into professions can be rationalized at least in part by the steady increase in the technical or theoretical component of modern work, although it is surely obvious that a number of the most recently established "professions" are merely ordinary jobs putting on airs. But there is no argument save historical accident for the practice of locating these professions institutionally in universities. The advantage to the new profession is obvious. If undertakers can persuade the state university to establish a degree—a *graduate* degree, yet!—in Mortuary Science, then they can wrap themselves quite literally in the robes of the academy, to the spiritual and financial benefit of the entire calling. But the question remains what effect is produced in the university by this endless expansion of its repertory of degrees, and what attitude we should take toward the process.

The easy and obvious attitude is an aristocratic disdain for whatever is new and vulgar. The faculty of arts and sciences looks with suspicion upon the candidates in law and medicine, who in turn feel an impatient irritation at the candidates for masters of art in teaching—the entire company of learned men averting its eyes as social work and library science receive their distinctive hoods. But though I find this attitude natural, holding as I do a degree in philosophy itself, the very original of the "academic" calling, still it seems to me a superficial response to a very deep problem. If I may make a rather odd comparison, it is like those liberal criticisms of American foreign policy during the Eisenhower years which made much of ineptitude of style and technique and ignored the more important question of basic goals. The fundamental question is not whether mortuary science should be granted a place alongside medicine, and library science next to law, but whether a university is an appropriate place for professional schools *at all*.

In the last chapter of this book, I shall argue for the Draconian proposal that *all* professional schools and professional degree-granting programs should be driven out of the university and forced to set themselves up as independent institutes. At this point, I wish merely to indicate some of the implications of professional training for the educational activities and institutional organization of a university.

The inclusion of professional schools and programs within the university damages and eventually destroys the unity of the academic community. Each professional school seeks to prepare its students for admission to the profession in the larger society. Hence, relationships develop which cut across university lines. The medical school establishes an association with a local hospital in which its students can do practical work. The professors maintain private medical practices as well as giving time to clinics. The faculty of the law school adjusts its curriculum to the demands of the state bar association, on whose committees many professors may sit. Practice teaching for education students requires a standing arrangement between the school of education and local primary- and secondary-school systems.

In countless ways, the activities of the professors and students of the professional schools reach out beyond the university, and inevitably loyalties are divided. The professional faculties cannot commit themselves or their energies to the university unconditionally, as professors in the arts and sciences regularly do. It was not surprising, therefore, that during the Columbia crisis, the college faculty and members of the graduate faculties of arts and sciences involved themselves most completely in the affair, while members of the law, medical, and business faculties rarely did more than attend the several large all-faculties meetings called by the president.

I do not see how the centrifugal dispersion of energies and loyalties can possibly be halted while professional schools and programs remain in the university community. It is obviously desirable that medical students spend time in hospital wards, that law professors help to set the standards of admission to the bar, that future teachers have the opportunity to conduct real classes under supervision before they begin their regular careers. And so long as such connections exist between sections of the university community and other social institutions, it will be impossible for the university itself to command the undivided loyalty and attention of all its members.*

Despite the fact that professional programs are tending more

---

* A second problem of great importance, though not directly relevant to our discussion, is the effect on the professions themselves of state regulations in the form of licensing boards, certification procedures, and legal codes of professional ethics. It might appear to be all to the good that the state should thus oversee the conduct of the professions, but a number of observers of quite diverse political persuasions have pointed out hidden dangers. Milton Friedman, in his iconoclastic essays *Capitalism and Freedom* (Chicago: University of Chicago Press, 1962, 1963), makes a striking attack on the state's regulation of the medical profession. By empowering boards of doctors to set quite high standards of medical education and qualification, Friedman argues, the state effectively divides the general population into two groups: those who can afford to pay for—and indeed get—generally excellent medical care, and those who, not being able to afford the medical care available, are also denied an opportunity to be treated by second-rate doctors with inferior medical preparation. By making "quacks" illegal, the state in effect says to the poor, "If you cannot afford the best, you must settle for nothing." Would we re-

and more to be located at the graduate level in American universities, professionalism has a very powerful effect on the character of undergraduate education. To some extent, this influence is felt whether the professional school is part of the university or not; but in some cases, as we shall see, the intrusion of professionalism into college education is helped along by the total lack of separation between undergraduate and professional curricula or faculties.

From the point of view of the professions, a college is expected to perform *three* functions: First, it must sort the undergraduates out into two groups—those who are acceptable as candidates for admission to professional programs and those who are unacceptable. Second, it must rank the acceptable candidates along a scale of excellence in aptitude and achievement in order to facilitate a fair and efficient distribution of scarce places in the more desirable professional programs (the crunch to get into Harvard Medical School is probably the most familiar example). And third, it must prepare undergraduates for professional training through inclusion in its curriculum of material which the professional schools wish to require as prerequisite to admission. The first two of these functions are inseparably bound up with the process of *grading*, a subject so complex and controversial that I shall deal with it in a separate section later in this book. The third touches upon the large question of the proper conduct and style of undergraduate education.

---

fuse to allow a poor man to buy a secondhand Ford, on the grounds that no one should drive less than a new Rolls-Royce?

From the other end of the political spectrum, Henry Kariel makes an extremely persuasive case for the repressive and establishmentarian effect of state certification in a number of professional fields. In his book, *The Decline of Pluralism* (Stanford: Stanford University Press, 1967), Kariel shows how the state strengthens the medical establishment of the AMA by placing in its hands the legal power to take away a dissident doctor's license, deprive him of indispensable hospital affiliation, and deny him the specialty certification he needs for certain sorts of medical practice.

Problems like these do not in the final instance concern the university, but insofar as professional faculties serve also on state licensing boards, the university becomes implicated in governmental activities which may very well limit its freedom as a community of free inquiry.

Three views of what undergraduate education ought to be are at work in America today, and corresponding to them are three sorts of undergraduate curricula. The first view is that college is merely an extension of high school—more material, a higher level of accomplishment demanded, somewhat greater freedom of choice and independence of work habits, but essentially just four more years of high school. The second view is that college is, or ought to be, the opening stage of professional training—in short, that college should really be graduate school. The proponents of this notion point to the improvements in high school preparation of today's college students and argue that the junior and senior years of college could be integrated into graduate and professional training programs with no educational loss and a great saving in time to the school-burdened student. The third view is that between the accumulation of knowledge and skills at the secondary level, and the professional preparation at the graduate level, there ought to occur an intellectual, cultural, and emotional experience which is *neither* a mere continuation of what went before *nor* a mere foretaste of what is to follow. Since I am deeply committed to a belief in the unique and irreducible character of undergraduate education, I should like to sketch a few arguments for it here and then try to show how the ideals and demands of professional training have invaded and at least partially destroyed it.

Sometime in late adolescence, boys and girls enter an extended period during which they make the difficult transition from childhood to the adult world. Just as the greater biological complexity of human beings lengthens and complicates the physical process of sexual maturation, producing the distinctive suspension of sexual development known in psychoanalytic theory as the latency period, so the complexity, flexibility, and autonomy of growing-up in our society produces the distinctive phase which Erikson calls the "identity crisis."

The child as a student masters a number of linguistic and mathematical skills and absorbs a body of information with very little psychic conflict.* But on the threshold of adulthood, he is

* Although quite unnecessary strain may be produced by familial and social pressure to do well in a competitive ranking system associated with the

suddenly faced with a problem much greater than any his schooling has ever posed. He must decide who he is, and hence who he is going to be for the rest of his life. He must choose not only a career, a job, an occupational role, but also a life-style, a set of values which can serve as his ideal self-image, and toward which he can grow through the commitment of his emotional energies. These choices are fateful, dangerous, highly charged, and are felt as such by the young man- or woman-to-be. Sexuality is of course an element in the emotional intensity of the choice, but it is by no means the most important. Ideology looms larger, as Erikson says. The very openness of choice in our society forces the late adolescent to question the deepest assumptions of his culture and upbringing. Hence religion in former times, and politics today, play a greater role than sex or money in the searching doubts of the future adult.

College is the appropriate setting for this transitional experience, and undergraduate education should be designed to facilitate and enrich it, not to squelch it. Ideally, students should be removed from their homes and gathered together into autonomous residential and educational communities. There they can experiment with being adult in a setting which is at once divorced from parental supervision (and the domination of the parent-child relationship) and somewhat insulated from the adult world of occupational roles and familial obligations. Through an education which is both exacting and flexible, students can make provisional commitments to styles of thought and action, test them for their fittingness, and either reject or adopt them in a more permanent way. I do not mean to imply that all students ought to become academics or intellectuals. But I do maintain that every young person should grow to adulthood with a style of intellect and sensibility which he has freely chosen in order to express his own needs, thoughts, and feelings in an appropriate and spontaneous

---

learning, children do not resist learning; what they frequently resist is the demand that they submit enthusiastically to invidious comparisons between themselves and their fellows.

way. The life of the intellectual is indeed only one among many, but the life of the mind should be the possession of every man and woman.

There are many readers, I fear, who will consider these remarks patronizing to undergraduates—the latest in a long line of rationalizations for the doctrine that the college stands *in loco parentis* to the student. Insofar as I deny that adulthood is the mere negation of childhood, I may indeed appear to patronize young people, for I admit that they are no longer children and yet refuse to acknowledge that they are adults. But this prolongation of the path to adulthood is the price we pay for the greater moral and spiritual autonomy that adulthood brings. There is no identity crisis for the child who has no freedom to choose an identity. The ancient Hebrews declared a boy to be a man at age twelve, and indeed, why not? He was not expected to *choose whether to be a Jew*; that was decided for him. When he could perform the predetermined roles assigned to him by his society, it was time for him to assume the status of an adult. The postponement of adulthood in our society is (or ought to be) a consequence of the weightiness of what it is to *be* an adult.

Educationally, the failure to recognize the unique importance of the transitional stage results in the attempt to hasten professional training. If no useful purpose is served by college, save as a brushup on high school subjects and a preparation for graduate school, then obviously one should improve high school education and start students on the road to their professions as early in their lives as possible. According to this view, undergraduate curricula should be reconstructed so that students need not waste time on irrelevant subjects or on introductory courses which will only have to be repeated at the graduate level. With appropriately "enriched" programs, we should be able to turn out lawyers at age twenty, doctors at age twenty-two, and doctors of philosophy at age twenty-four. Just such proposals are increasingly popular in American educational circles today. They place an especially high premium on early choice of career. The ideal student, in the eyes of such educators, is not the enthusiastic and imaginative young man or woman who vigorously challenges the norms and roles offered by society, but the college freshman who already knows the topic of his doctoral dissertation. Surely it is not difficult to see that the precocious student, by moving smoothly from secondary schooling to professional training, loses precisely that experience of choice and commitment which is a precondition of genuine moral and emotional freedom.

To be sure, the transitional period is unruly, awkward, marked by false starts, shifts of direction, and dramatic changes of emotional climate. To the mature adult, a young student in the full flush of an identity crisis is at the very least an embarrassment and at the worst a threatening reminder of the compromises and dissatisfactions which lie beneath the surface of his own settled life. Frequently, therefore, students find their natural allies among the ranks of those men and women who feel a need to remain suspended, as it were, in an incompletely resolved crisis of identity. Such adults are frequently the very best undergraduate teachers, and in a college setting they find a social use for a psychological condition which would be merely a hindrance elsewhere in society.

Given this conception of undergraduate education, it seems to me that college could fruitfully begin earlier and perhaps not last quite so long. A practical proposal, responsive to the pressures of professionalization and to the present structure of secondary education, would be to admit students to college at the end of their eleventh year, for a college program of three years' duration. There should be *no* preprofessional training during that three years, although students ought to be permitted to *concentrate* their studies in any way they wish. Then, those students wishing to go on to graduate and professional programs would do so, pausing perhaps, as in the case of medicine, for a year of concentrated preparation in the special subjects required by their chosen profession. By means of this arrangement, the three stages of education would be clearly distinguished, and the crucial second stage would be given a separate institutional setting at just the right time in the lives of the students. No one would be led to confuse specialization with professionalism, or career uncertainty with unseriousness and weakness of will.

Opponents of professionalization at the undergraduate level

have frequently supported their position by appeals to theories of the nature of the subject matter of education. As we have already remarked, it is common to invoke the great cultural tradition which is the common heritage of all educated men, and then to identify the undergraduate years as the appropriate time for transmitting this tradition to students. At some institutions, so mechanical was the application of this view that a student was permitted to acquire his first degree merely by passing a set of survey examinations in the great tradition (University of Chicago under Hutchins). Elsewhere, emphasis was laid on reading the great books in their original languages (St. John's), or on mastering the historical sweep of the tradition (Columbia).

"Interdisciplinary studies" and "problem orientation" have also appeared as slogans on the placards of the antiprofessionals. The enemy here is "specialization," which is considered the characteristic vice of the professional. Cross-disciplinary curricula, staff-taught courses drawing on the faculties of several departments, undergraduate major fields defined in terms of problems rather than disciplines, all have been tried as ways of differentiating undergraduate from graduate education and ensuring that professional training is postponed until after the bachelor's degree.*

There is no reason why undergraduate education should not embody a theory about intellectual traditions or about the value of nonspecialization, so long as the members of the faculty are committed to it and the students responsive to it. But as a defense against professionalization, such a maneuver originates in a confusion. The distinguishing mark of professional training is not its *content* but its *form* (if I may adapt an old philosophical distinction). Professional training aims at the achievement of *qualification*, through the demonstrated mastery of a body of material and a repertory of skills. It is infused with the distinctive norms of the profession, which the candidate is expected to internalize and conform to. The candidate's social role, status, income, and, to a considerable extent, self-image will be defined by the profes-

---

* Needless to say, both interdisciplinary studies and problem-oriented programs have flourished at the graduate level, particularly in the natural and social sciences.

sion for which he prepares himself. These characteristics of professional training, and not the degree of generality or specificity of the material learned, set professional training off from other forms of education. A general practitioner is as thoroughly professionalized as a heart specialist. City planners, for all the extraordinary breadth of their field, are professionals, and as for the great tradition, prerevolutionary China has demonstrated that even a humanistic education can be molded into professional training.

I myself am a devoted admirer of the great tradition, a long-time practitioner of the arts of disciplinary cross-fertilization—and yet, I would be perfectly happy to see an undergraduate devote himself enthusiastically to the study of a narrow, ahistorical speciality. Precision, detail, sophistication, a concentration on the particular, are as valuable in intellectual activity as breadth, perspective, synthesis, and a sense of the whole. What matters is that the material should engage the student's intellect and sensibility, that he should be held to the highest possible standards of thought, and that his activity be free of the extraneous career consequences of the professional school. Only by such genuine experimentation, sharply different from both the dilettante's superficiality and the professional's career commitment, can a young man discover who he is and who he wants to be.

Before leaving the subject of professionalism in higher education, we must take a look at the anomalous case of the *academic profession*, which occupies a special and peculiar position in the university. The academic profession is in a manner of speaking the proprietor of the university, its natural inhabitant. The university is to professors what the hospital is to doctors or the courts to lawyers. And yet, it seems odd to call professors professionals at all, despite the fact that their very title proclaims that status. Using the term in its modern sociological sense, rather than in the original meaning as "one who professes [some doctrine]," can we correctly describe university professors as *professional men?* And if we can, what ought the relationship be of this profession to the university?

A university professor's work characteristically consists of two distinct and sometimes conflicting activities. First of all, he regularly engages in some sort of creative intellectual work, whether scientific research, literary analysis, pure mathematics, social criticism, or classical scholarship. Intellectual creation *as such* is not the distinctive activity of any particular social or occupational role, although a society may institutionalize certain features of it in an attempt to transform it into a defined role. In the history of Western civilization, at least, amateurs have contributed as much as professionals to the sciences, arts, and human disciplines. In the earliest days of philosophy, for example, it was considered a mark of moral superiority not to earn any money from one's philosophizing. Plato, Descartes, Spinoza, Locke, and Marx are among the great philosophers who cannot be said to have lived off their philosophy, while St. Thomas, Rousseau, Hume, Kant, Hegel, and Russell in some sense did. It would be impossible to find any indication of this difference in the philosophical theories actually espoused by members of the two groups.

The difference between intellectual creation and professional activity is vested in a distinction deeper than that between the professional and the amateur. The significant point is not the economic payoff of the activity, but the nature of the criteria or standards against which it is measured. Intellectual creations are judged by the criterion of *truth*, by which I mean not only fidelity to reality but also theoretical simplicity, explanatory power, conceptual elegance, and logical coherence. After everything has been granted which must be granted to the sociology of knowledge, the fact remains that the criteria of success in historical research or philosophical argument are *not* socially defined. It would make perfectly good sense to say that the entire scientific population of a society was engaged in bad or wrong research, or that all of the mathematics done in a society was inconsistent. Intellectual creation, in short, is not at base a *social* activity, despite the fact that it is frequently done by groups of men, at the instigation of society, and for social rewards.

Professions, on the other hand, are social roles whose content and significance are defined by norms operative in the society.*

* As defined in this way, some professions include a nonprofessional component whose correct analysis involves extra-social considerations. Medicine,

There are no objective correlates to the professional activity of the lawyer, the accountant, or the priest (assuming for the moment that there is no God). Even the architect and the general pursue careers whose criteria of success are social in origin, for what counts as good housing or military victory is a matter of culture, not nature. Hence, the university professor is *not* properly a professional insofar as he engages in intellectual or artistic creation.

As an active participant in some form of intellectual activity, the professor characteristically takes upon himself the responsibility for initiating others into the traditions and forms of the activity.* He is thus *teacher* as well as *creator*. The relationship of professor to student in this initiation is rather like that of master to apprentice. The two seek one another out freely and establish a bond, by mutual agreement, which is moral and emotional as well as intellectual. The apprentice-master relation is most obvious in scientific laboratories, whose one senior chemist or biologist will preside over a complex of research activities carried on by students and junior scientists, much as a medieval master craftsman would oversee a small family of apprentices and journeymen. Something like the same instruction should occur between a doctoral candidate and the director of his dissertation, although of course it frequently doesn't.

But graduate education has a professional as well as a nonprofes-

---

for example, seeks to cure physical ailments. Since it is a natural, not a social, fact whether someone is sick, doctors obviously conform their activities at least in part to natural, as opposed to social, standards. Thus, an educated layman who performs successful operations while passing himself off as a certified surgeon can be said genuinely to have cured illness, but not thereby to have shown himself to be a qualified doctor. A poet, on the other hand, has in our society no professional setting for his activity. Hence, it would be meaningless to speak of someone successfully "impersonating" a poet by writing good poems while not being correctly certified. One of the peculiar side effects of excessive professionalization in American society is the tendency of academics to look on amateur historians or philosophers as impostors, as though only a man with a Ph.D. should be permitted to try his hand at *professional* scholarship!

* My discussion of this process of initiation very much reflects the sensitive account given by Michael Oakeshott in his collection of essays, *Rationalism in Politics* (New York: Basic Books, 1962).

sional component. The professional component is the procedure of certification, leading characteristically to the conferring of a degree. It is governed by norms of competence, fairness, and objectivity which have little to do with original intellectual creativity. The professors in a graduate department are expected to suspend their personal intellectual convictions when passing on the performances of doctoral candidates. The same logical positivist who regularly follows Hume's injunction to "consign to the flames" any books containing nonempirical metaphysics is expected to sit impartially on the board of a candidate who has written in the style of Hegel. To be sure, professors frequently fall short of this professional norm of objectivity, but they acknowledge themselves bound by it nonetheless, just as fee splitters pay lip service to the Hippocratic oath. Politically motivated favoritism or reprisal is considered a particularly serious violation of professional norms in academic circles. However difficult he may find the effort, a professor must not allow the political persuasions of the student to influence his judgment in the processes of certification. One measure of the intensity of the passions stirred up on the Columbia campus, I regret to say, was the inability of a small number of distinguished professors to abide by this inflexible principle of professional life.

The nonprofessional component in graduate education is the intellectual, emotional, and moral interaction through which a student learns from a professor what it is to be a creative intellect. There are no socially determined rules in this relationship, no prerequisites, certifications, or degrees. No act of a university can confer intellectual creativity on a professor who lacks it, and no law can compel a student to enter into a relationship which he resists or condemns.

The conflict between professional certification and intellectual initiation destroys the coherence of graduate education in American universities. At every turn, professors and students find themselves torn by the contradictory standards and divergent demands of the two activities. The result has been to make the process of certification needlessly painful and to corrupt the process of initiation.

Consider, for example, the requirements for the degree of Doctor of Philosophy. At most American universities, the candidate must complete a set of courses and examinations designed to demonstrate his mastery of the content and techniques of a defined field of knowledge. He must then present an extended piece of writing which purports to contain an "original contribution to knowledge." Now, every professor who has ever attempted to administer this system of requirements knows that there is something wrong with them—which he expresses, typically, by the complaints that "standards are too low," and that "students take too long to get through." But very few academics perceive that the source of the problem is the conflict between the ideals or criteria of certification and initiation.

Certification is the maintaining and applying of public, objective, impartial, minimal standards of competence. It is a species of what I have called *evaluation*. When a law faculty certifies a candidate in law, or a medical faculty a candidate in medicine, it attests that the candidate has demonstrated at least a specified minimal command of the discipline (of course, the minimal level may be quite high). In its certification procedures, the faculty openly appeals to the accepted norms of the profession; but it is pledged not to impose on candidates its particular convictions with regard to matters which are subjects of dispute within the profession. Thus, a law professor ought not to fail a student who disagrees with him on the matter of loose versus strict construction of the Constitution, but he may perfectly well fail a student who refuses to master the rules of evidence on the grounds that legal disputes should be decided in trial by combat. Nor need a mathematics professor feel any compunction about failing a candidate who disdains consistency as the hobgoblin of little minds.

Furthermore, since certification is a social precondition of employment in the profession, students acquire certain economic or quasi-economic rights which the faculty is bound to honor. If a graduate student completes the course and examination requirements for the doctorate at a fully acceptable level of performance, he has a *right* to begin work on his dissertation under the direction of some qualified member of his department. He may be a tedious person, the members of the faculty may all have other interests and projects, no professor may feel moved to take the student on—no matter. The candidate has a right to dissertation direction and the faculty has a duty to provide it. This obligation is as binding on the academic profession as is the doctor's duty to continue the treatment of his patient. To recognize and honor such obligations is a very large part of what it is to be a professional.

But the standard of adequacy in the writing of the dissertation —"an original contribution to knowledge"—*is not a standard of minimal professional competence and cannot in all honesty be administered as such.* Disputes over the genuine originality and significance of a putative contribution to a field of knowledge are precisely the sorts of disputes which arise *between* reputable members of the academic profession. Such disputes appeal to the objective criterion of truth, rather than to the socially defined criterion of professional competence. Intellectuals repeatedly condemn, as worthless, pieces of work which, in their role as professors, they would readily accept as competent doctoral dissertations. Members of the same department, who privately view each other's intellectual creations as completely without value, must sit together on doctoral committees and somehow transform the intellectual standard of "contribution to knowledge" into a professional standard of competence.

The conflicts begin well before the dissertation stage is reached. As creative intellects initiating others into their activity, professors quite naturally feel a powerful desire to turn away all but the very few students who show genuine signs of talent and a deep personal commitment to the creative enterprise. But as the certifying officials of their profession, these same professors consider themselves bound to respond to the pressures of the profession as a whole. Graduate programs expand to meet the demand for Ph.D.'s, not in response to the arrival at their doors of greater numbers of brilliant students. It is as though Jascha Heifetz were to schedule extra masterclasses because the New York Philharmonic had empty desks in the second violin section!

Internal institutional contradictions are no doubt distressing to philosophers, who have a professional penchant for vesting logic with metaphysical significance. But for the social critic, the crucial question must be *cui male?* Who is hurt by the situation? I am persuaded that both students and professors are hurt, in their certification activities as well as in their relationship as teacher and student.

The greatest source of harm is the dissertation requirement imposed on every doctoral candidate. Graduate students by and large find the course and examination requirements similar to the sorts of work they handled successfully as undergraduates. Standards are higher, and the professional commitment demanded of them is exceedingly threatening to some candidates who until then have relied for inspiration on no more than a natural enthusiasm for the field; but graduate schools do not find it difficult to devise a system of qualifying requirements which their students can handle. At the dissertation stage, on the other hand, candidates linger painfully for years. Outsiders are always astonished to discover the *average* time required for the completion of the Ph.D. It is common for eight, ten, twelve, or more years to elapse between the candidate's enrollment and the awarding of the degree. Most of this time is spent working on the dissertation. No one will ever total up the marriages ruined, the children neglected, the anguish suffered, and the years of fruitful work blighted by the curse of the unfinished dissertations. As a young faculty member at Harvard and Chicago, I frequently found myself serving on the examination committees of men ten years my senior, whose length of teaching experience far exceeded my own.

It is not hard to discover the source of the problem. The doctoral dissertation is supposed to be precisely *not* the sort of task which a competent student of the subject can set for himself in a limited period of time. The dissertation is *not* five, or eight, or fifteen term papers. It is supposed to be in some way an *original* piece of creative work. Now, no one would think of trying to set a timetable for creative work. It would be absurd to suggest that Kant was somehow remiss in waiting eleven years after his Inaugural Dissertation before publishing the *Critique of Pure Reason*. Indeed, it is usually counted to his credit that he chose to withhold publication until he had solved the deep problems which stood in his way. But the doctoral candidate is urged, cajoled, seduced, and pressured to finish his dissertation quickly. He is told to take a "manageable" topic, limit it rigorously, work efficiently —and produce something original and worthwhile! Perhaps Johann Sebastian Bach could turn the chore of composing a weekly cantata into the act of creating beautiful music, but even most geniuses find it difficult to make so great a virtue of necessity.

The natural response to the destructive anomalies of the Ph.D. is to lower both sights and standards. Don't attempt an original and creative work, the candidate is told. Do something merely different and competent. Edit a text too obscure to have caught another scholar's eye; survey the complete works of a minor figure justly forgotten; ring one more change on some old ideas which have not suffered *every* possible permutation as yet.

Surely it is obvious that no good can come of such a system. Those few candidates who have the seeds of creation within them will be blighted by the necessity of contorting their original thoughts into the unnatural shape of the dissertation. The others, competent though they are to master their field and teach it, are compelled to drag out of themselves the simulacrum of a new idea, wasting their energies and, like as not, destroying their enthusiasm for their chosen subject.

In the last chapter, I shall propose a radical reconstruction of graduate education designed to eliminate these wasteful efforts and establish a rational system of professional training and certification. At this point, I wish only to lay bare the source of the trouble. To repeat, the incoherence of graduate education arises from the conflict between two distinct activities guided by two entirely separate sets of standards, namely, the training and certification of college teachers on the one hand, and the initiation of promising acolytes into intellectual creativity on the other. Insofar as the standards of the first are inappropriately applied to the products of the second, the current student outcry against "professionalism" has a legitimate basis in fact.

CHAPTER THREE

The University as a Social Service Station

Our third model is at once a description, a prediction, and a justification. It portrays the university as a complex institution, or perhaps an aggregation of institutions loosely held together, which performs an array of educational, research, consultative, and other services for American society as a whole. The theorist of this model is of course Dr. Clark Kerr, former President of the University of California, whose Godkin Lectures at Harvard in 1963, published under the title *The Uses of the University*, have given us the indispensable term "multiversity."

Kerr's book is one of those rare productions which, in its fusion of style and argument, form and content, perfectly exemplifies its subject of discourse. Eclectic, pragmatic, thoroughly modern in diction as in thought, *The Uses of the University* is somehow just the sort of book which *ought* to be written by the president of a multiversity. It is couched in "descriptive-celebratory" style, as we may call the ambiguous cross between factual narration and normative defense which so many of our social scientists adopt when speaking of contemporary American institutions. One is never entirely clear whether Dr. Kerr is merely recounting the changes which he perceives in American universities or congratulating us all on them. Nevertheless, I think we can easily enough separate the description and prediction from the justification and consider them in isolation.

"Today," Kerr begins, "the large American university is . . . a whole series of communities and activities held together by a common name, a common governing board, and related purposes." It is, as he puts it, a "Federal Grant university," for its financing, its direction of growth, its purposes, and its personnel are all dominated by the availability of federal support, in the form of research grants, student fellowships, aid to area studies or language programs, funds for laboratory construction, and so forth.

The multiversity, as its name suggests, exhibits none of the unity of place, purpose, and political organization which characterized older universities. At its heart lies an undergraduate college—or perhaps many undergraduate colleges and programs. But it stretches out in every direction, embracing professional schools, research institutes, training programs, hospitals, primary and secondary schools, farms and laboratories, in several cities, states, even in other countries. The University of California will probably have a branch operation on the moon before the century is out.

The ancient image of the walled enclave is of course entirely inappropriate to the modern multiversity, which has no walls or gates, and so cannot even be said to "stand open" to the larger society. It simply merges with its surroundings, so that even at the level of budgets and administration it may be difficult to discern the precise boundaries of the institution. Of all the interpenetrations, that between multiversity and federal government is most significant. So completely have the two come to rely upon one another that the relationship might better be considered a symbiosis than a seduction. The movement of men from classroom to government bureau to university administration and back is steady and unimpeded. The paths beaten by these traveling experts are soon followed by students, who go easily from a graduate program in political science to a congressional internship, back to take a doctorate and on to the State Department or Pentagon, and back again to the university; the phrase "circulation of elites," had it not already been preempted in sociology for a somewhat different phenomenon, would perfectly characterize the flow of personnel between government and multiversity.

Like all social institutions which undergo rapid change, the multiversity exhibits a considerable incoherence between its new, expanding programs and its sizable body of established, traditional activities. The president may concentrate his attention on the new institutes, grants, programs, and degrees which spring up on the periphery of the institutions; but there will still be many professors and students whose lives are untouched by these "multiversitarian" activities. To the member of the more traditional humanities departments, for example, the only effects may be a rash of new building in the vicinity and the subtle awareness that elsewhere in the university faculty members are paid better and students receive fatter fellowships. As is well known, the natural sciences are most thoroughly at home with the new order, the humanities least comfortable (save for certain formerly quite arcane languages which have suddenly acquired "strategic" value), with the social sciences ranging themselves between the two poles. Some very anomalous marriages and arrangements take place, testifying (according to one's prejudices) either to the open-minded liberality or mindless stupidity of the federal government. One of the most prominent radical critics of American foreign policy, for example, draws much of his substantial pay from a federal grant to an electronics laboratory, where he does brilliant work on—of all things—the philosophy of language. A second flourishes as a professor of industrial engineering in a university division which depends upon government grants.

The multiversity is not a mere receiver of social benefits, the terminus of a flow of social wealth. It is itself a highly productive element of the American economy through its training of skilled personnel, its development of new technology, and the accumulation in its faculty of scarce and much-desired expertise. Kerr repeats the familiar observation that California, New York, and Massachusetts have taken disproportionate shares of defense contracts and industrial development because of their congeries of academic institutions. We see here a vivid evidence of the fact that technical knowledge is an even more valuable economic resource than mineral deposits in an advanced industrial society. It is easier and cheaper to bring the raw materials for electronics industries to Boston than it would be to induce the scientists of MIT or Harvard to move, say, to Minnesota.

Like the great conglomerate corporations which have grown up through mergers, takeovers, and diversification, the multiversities become involved in virtually every sort of activity requiring technical expertise or bookish skills. They are the holding companies of the knowledge industry. The criterion of admission to the multiversity, however, is not profitability in the economic sense but profitability in the social sense. The multiversities become social service stations.

It is not difficult to articulate the argument which can be made in favor of the multiversity. To begin with, the multiversity is not unique in serving the ends of the larger society. As Kerr points out, universities have always devoted themselves to purposes at least partially defined by social forces and social groups outside the walls, whether by glorifying God, training ministers, preparing the sons of the upper classes for positions of rule, or turning out the experts needed to run a technological economy. In a democratic and pluralist age, it is only natural that those demands should be many, varied, even conflicting. To meet them, the institution must itself become internally diverse, quite probably at the price of the unity and harmony which graced an earlier age. The critic who bemoans the loss of institutional community is really asking that only a single social interest be served in the university. No matter which interest is chosen, the result must be counted a loss to all but a fraction of the society as a whole. In this way, academic radicals manage to combine an extreme egalitarianism in politics with a reactionary elitism in education. The true defender of democratic values (I trust the reader will recall that I am still rehearsing the defense of the multiversity) is the dedicated and harried multiversity president, through whose tactful maneuvering the widest array of conflicting interests are accommodated within the academy. Here is Kerr describing the office of which he was the first occupant:

> The president in the multiversity is leader, educator, creator, initiator, wielder of power, pump; he is *also* office holder, caretaker, inventor, consensus-seeker, persuader, bottleneck. But he is mostly a mediator [p. 36].

Social justice, as well as history, requires the university to serve the society in which it resides. It is, after all, parisitic upon the community, consuming resources much as monasteries once did. The social bookkeeping may be a trifle obscure, but somewhere, somehow, the professors and students are living off the productive labor of the working classes. And the purer, the more intellectually meritorious the activities of the academy, the more thoroughly they are parisitic. Surely it is reasonable that the recipients of this benefaction should return a part of its value to the society in the form of technological innovation, expert consulting, professional training, and cooperation in socially useful enterprises. However dedicated the public may be to the religion of education, with its magnificent temples, ancient texts, exclusive rituals, and conspicuously idle priests, there is a limit to the amount of wealth the academy may legitimately absorb in a society far from affluent.

It is not only traditional *and* just that the university serve society; it is also exceedingly useful that it do so. As a people, we Americans are active rather than contemplative. When we have identified a social evil, our inclination is to do something about it, not to reflect on its significance for the human condition. At every level of the public and private sectors we are busy planning, adjusting, experimenting. There is an insatiable need for expert knowledge and advice, and the universities are great social repositories of such expertise. It is as wasteful for a great university to sit untapped in the midst of a modern city as it would be for the Colorado to flow on undammed or the Mesabi to lie unexploited. There is not an enterprise in America, from the formulating of foreign policy to the organizing of community control of public schools, which does not benefit from the active participation of the personnel of the multiversity.

If tradition, justice, and social utility are not sufficient to justify the multiversity, let us add one final argument: in a society which distributes wealth and status very unequally indeed, the multiversity serves as a prime instrument of opportunity and upward mobility for millions of Americans who would otherwise be trapped at the lower levels of the social pyramid. The great English, French, and German universities have been exclusive institutions where high and specialized standards of admissions effectively barred all but the privileged few. Whether by the economic inutility of their courses of instruction, the unavailability of the dead languages they demanded of applicants, the rigidity of their standards, or even merely by their expense, they effectively guaranteed that only the sons of the wealthy and well-placed would matriculate within their walls. By contrast, the multiversity opens its arms to students from virtually every level of wealth, social status, and native ability. Through networks of community colleges and adult education programs, it draws in students who either cannot afford, cannot handle, or would never have thought to seek, a traditional four-year degree in arts and sciences. The poorly prepared student, the under achiever, the late developer, are encouraged to slip almost imperceptibly into the orbit of the multiversity. The ablest among them are there spotted by their teachers and encouraged to advance to the next level of academic achievement. At Columbia University, for example, there are men in the faculty who began in the School of General Studies and were brought along through graduate study to the Ph.D. Had the system been forced to make a final decision on them in their undergraduate days, they would undoubtedly have been rejected and lost to Columbia.

The same openness can be seen in the multiversity's willingness to add degree-granting programs in subjects once decisively excluded from the academic world. The haughty humanist may consider nursing or landscape gardening lesser breeds without the law, but how many young people would never have any experience whatever of the life of a university if they were forced to take the quadrivium and trivium or nothing at all! One need simply look at the university systems of France or England to see the destructive social effects of an elitist philosophy of education.

We can conclude this defense of the multiversity with a passage from Kerr. Characteristically, Kerr insists that he speaks *descriptively*, but the tone is clearly celebratory:

The American University is currently undergoing its second great transformation. The first occurred during roughly the last quarter of the nineteenth century, when the land grant movement and German intellectualism were together bringing extraordinary change. The current transformation will cover roughly the quarter century after World War II. The university is being called upon to educate previously unimagined numbers of students; to respond to the expanding claims of national service; to merge its activities with industry as never before; to adapt to and rechannel new intellectual currents. By the end of this period, there will be a truly American university, an institution unique in world history, an institution not looking to other models but serving, itself, as a model for universities in other parts of the globe [p. 86].

I think we may say that we have given the multiversity a fair hearing. It has tradition behind it, justice and utility for it, and the future ahead of it. Why then does the prospect of it so depress us? Why does every right-thinking (which is to say, left-leaning) reader turn in dismay from Kerr's description? What, as the English rather quaintly say, is so off-putting about the multiversity?

There are four grounds for this reaction to the emergence of the multiversity, of which one is in my opinion illegitimate, a second legitimate but relatively unimportant, and two so important that together they outweigh the genuinely powerful justification which we have just sketched.

In academic circles, the principal source of anti-multiversity feeling seems to be mere intellectual snobbism. Aristocrats are characteristically sentimental about the poor and contemptuous of the middle class. So it is in academia. The same Ivy League brahmins who welcome the disadvantaged and the ghetto dweller into their midst, scorn the business courses, nursing program, extension schools, and institutes of applied expertise which constitute the bourgeoisie of the intellectual world. The humanities and pure sciences look down on all those academic *arrivistes* who seem so perfectly at home in the multiversity. The ambition to turn a job into a profession seems comical to those who prefer to forget that their profession is also a job. The attitude of the academic elite to the multiversity is rather like that of eighteenth-century landed interests to monied interests, or—somewhat later—like that of old money to new money. As usual, this snobbery is tricked out in an ideology of scholarship and education, but beneath the rationalizations one can discern the same disdain which the aristo-

crat Plato expressed, 2500 years ago, for those Greek teachers who
charged money for their lessons.

A *legitimate* complaint against the multiversity is its tendency
to undermine the internal political organization of the academy.
For reasons which will be set forth in Part Three of this essay, I
share the widespread commitment to a faculty-student-run university. But my experiences at Columbia and elsewhere make me
very much aware of the difficulty of preserving genuine faculty-
student authority in an institution with many faculties, many student bodies, and no coherent bonds of internal unity. Even in a
traditional university there are centrifugal forces which tend to
separate department from department and division from division.
The sheer size of many university faculties makes the delegation of
authority appear inevitable. Under these circumstances, academic
institutions should move toward smaller units with more complete
autonomy of such discrete units as a medical school, law school, or
theological faculty. But the multiversity moves in precisely the
opposite direction. The more numerous and diverse the activities
it draws within its orbit, the more it must rely for its governance
on a central administration. When an affair like the Columbia uprising occurs, faculty and students are appalled to discover how
many of the activities of the university take place absolutely at the
discretion of the president or chancellor, without even the sem-
blance of control by the members of the university. Now, so long
as the university clings to its traditional form, the faculty and
students have some chance, however remote, of taking effective
collective control. But in the multiversity it is impossible even to
determine who should count as a member of the faculty or as a
student. In this organizational chaos, the central administration
rules, by default, as a responsive and benevolent dictator. Naturally, the multiversity president sees himself as more acted upon
than acting, powerless rather than powerful. But in fact, what
real power of decision there is in the multiversity concerning the
major questions of growth, financing, and so forth rests with him.
Dr. Kerr is quite right in comparing the role of multiversity president with that of President of the United States. Both are posi-

tions of rulership by default which bear no recognizable relation to the traditional ideals of democratic society.

But this is a minor evil of the multiversity. If nothing worse could be said against it, we would have to conclude that the benefits of the new university outweighed its faults. A very much deeper criticism must be made of the rationale of the multiversity, what Kant would have called its Regulative Principle of Action. The key to this principle is the slippery notion of "social need."

Throughout his essay, Kerr speaks of the multiversity as responding to social needs or as satisfying demands made upon it by society. Here are a few passages which echo this refrain:

> It is interesting that American universities . . . which are part of a highly decentralized and varied system of higher education should, nevertheless, have responded with such fidelity and alacrity to national *needs* [p. 49].

> Federal agencies are more responsive to particular *national needs* than the universities would be . . . [p. 59].

> With all its problems, however, federal research aid to universities has helped greatly in meeting national *needs* [p. 68].

> The nation *needs* more research activity . . . and more personnel. . . . From now to 1970 the expected supply of engineers and scientists will fill only three quarters of the *demand* [p. 76].

> Knowledge is exploding along with population. There is also an explosion in the *need* for certain skills. The university is responding to all these explosions. The vastly increased *needs* for engineers, scientists, and doctors will draw great resources to these areas of the university [pp. 110–111].
> [all emphases added]

The difficulty with these and countless other assertions in Kerr's book is their complete failure to draw a sharp distinction between the concepts of *effective or market demand* and *human or social need.* Dr. Kerr's discussion commits exactly the same error which lies at the heart of classical laisser-faire economic theory. In this way, his book serves as a perfect expression of liberal ideology.

The point is a simple one and many critics since Marx have elaborated it: A *human or social need* is a want, a lack, the absence of something material or social, whose presence would contribute to physical and emotional health, to the full and un-alienated development of human power—in a word, to true happiness. Individuals have needs for food, for leisure, for privacy, for the esteem of their fellows, for productive and fulfilling work. Societies of men have collective needs, for social justice, for peace, for cultural and political community.* Some needs are *felt needs* —that is to say, they are lacks or wants of which the needy persons are quite conscious. Other needs may not be *felt* as such, because of ignorance, or lack of experience. A man who has never experienced art in any form can hardly be expected to know that his life lacks one of the great fulfillments available to us, but it is perfectly possible for an external observer to see the drabness of his life and perceive what is missing. In the same way, a primitive tribe forever living on the edge of subsistence may have no idea what the human body can become, given good food, rest, and healthful exercise. Yet a doctor might easily observe that the entire tribe suffered a physiological lack, of vitamins perhaps, or protein, or sheer calories. In short, the distinction between felt and unfelt (or manifest and latent) need is empirically grounded; it requires no appeal to a theory of the "real self" or such like implausibilities of Idealist metaphysics.

Effective or market demand, on the other hand, is simply the existence in a market economy of buyers who are in the market place, have money in hand, and are prepared to spend it for a particular commodity. Hence the familiar expression, "He is in the market for" this or that. Demand is said to be *effective* when it is capable of eliciting a response in the form of a *supply.* Needless to say, there may be a large effective demand for a commodity at one price, and little or no effective demand for the same commodity at

* See Chapter Five, "Community," of my *The Poverty of Liberalism* (Boston: Beacon Press, 1968), for an analysis of the nature and varieties of community.

a higher price. Originally, the concept of effective demand was defined for the situation of a commodity market, but it is not difficult to see how it can be generalized. In the academic world, for example, when there are many applicants (large supply) for a few teaching positions (small effective demand), those doing the hiring can get away with a kind of callous mistreatment (broken promises, unanswered letters, discourteous interviews) which disappears as soon as the supply shrinks or the demand increases. That is why it is a good deal more pleasant to look for an academic position in California than in Boston or New York City. The "law of the market" even applies in affairs of the heart, as the scarce males at a summer resort can testify.

The rationale of the classical free market rests on two assumptions, both of which have for quite a long time now been known to be wrong. The first assumption is that all human and social needs are *felt needs*. The second assumption is that felt needs in a free market society are always expressible as *effective demand*. Thus, if men *need* food, they *feel* hungry. If they *feel* hungry, then they go into the market to *buy* food. The demand for food drives up the price, which drives up the profit, which attracts investors, who increase the supply, which drives down the price again *and satisfies the need*. A continuing rolling adjustment of resources to needs takes place, in a way which guarantees the fullest satisfaction possible with the resources and technology available.

In the classical theory, no moral judgments are permitted concerning "true" versus "false" needs, or "higher" versus "lower" pleasures. Happiness is assumed to be the only thing intrinsically good; and happiness, it is supposed, consists in the satisfaction of whatever desires one actually has. So when men want poetry, their expressed demand will elicit poetry from some source or other in society; when they want pornography, pornography will appear.

There is a case to be made for this pristine doctrine, although I confess that it has always seemed to me more aesthetically pleasing by virtue of its simplicity, than persuasive or plausible. But quite frequently, an author will appear who systematically identifies *effective market demand* with *true human need*, while not subscribing at all to the postulates and presuppositions which, as we have seen, underlie such an identification. That is, he will talk as though a demand in the market automatically expressed a human or social need, while at the same time talking as though he made moral judgments about true versus false needs. The result is not an argument, nor is it exactly just a confusion. The result is a covert ideological rationalization for whatever human or social desires happen to be backed by enough money or power to translate them into effective demands. I shall try briefly to show that Clark Kerr is guilty of exactly just such ideological rhetoric.

The crucial point is that many human needs cannot get themselves expressed adequately as market demands. In America, for example, there is a great need for cheap, well-made, well-designed clothing and housing. For a variety of technical reasons, it is possible to make a very nice profit from cheap, well-made, well-designed clothing. Hence, Americans by and large are well and attractively clothed at virtually every economic level save the very lowest. At the same time, little or no profit is to be made in well-designed, well-constructed, low-cost housing, although high-cost housing returns a fine profit. Here an enormous human and social need fails to express itself in a market demand capable of eliciting an adequate flow of investment capital, and our cities sink deeper and deeper into decay. The same disparity between *need* and *supply* exists in the field of medicine and public health, ghetto education, conservation, and pollution control.*

When Kerr speaks repeatedly of the multiversity's responsiveness to national *needs,* he is describing nothing more than its tendency to adjust itself to effective *demand* in the form of government grants, scholarship programs, corporate or alumni underwriting, and so forth. But his language encourages the reader to suppose that the demands to which the multiversity responds are

* In fairness to the laisser-faire position, which I have dismissed a bit casually, it ought to be pointed out that a major obstacle to the flow of capital and labor into such areas as medicine and low-cost housing is the existence of arbitrary restrictions (building codes, minimum-wage laws, medical licensing procedures) which violate the principle of the free market. I don't believe that these deviations from laisser-faire explain away the major failings of the capitalist system, but a good deal more argument than I have offered here would be necessary to refute such theorists as Milton Friedman.

expressions of genuine human and social needs, needs which make a moral claim upon the effort and attention of the academy. It takes very little thought to see the weakness of this implicit claim.

The nation *needs* more engineers and scientists, Kerr says. Only three fourths of the *demand* will be met at current rates of enroll-ment. But the shortage of engineers in America is due entirely to the enormous space program, which absorbs tens of thousands of highly trained personnel in an enterprise of very dubious social priority. When Kerr speaks of the "demand" for engineers as one to which the multiversity ought to respond, he is covertly (and probably unwittingly) endorsing the space program. He would hardly view the matter that way, I should imagine. But the alterna-tive is to assume without question that the multiversity should accept the goals and values of whoever in America has the money to pay for them. Instead of calling his essay *The Uses of the Uni-versity,* he could more appropriately have titled it *University for Hire!*

The same covert rationalization applies to the multiversity's ac-ceptance of war-related research. When Congress appropriates money for research into weapons systems, counterinsurgency tech-nology, or problems of manpower recruitment, that merely proves —at best—that the American people through their representatives wish to express a market *demand* for such research. To go a step further and say that such research meets a national *need* is to *endorse* the purposes to which it will be put, *approve* of them, adopt them as one's own. By systematically confusing the concepts of need and demand, Clark Kerr begs all of the major political questions of the day.

Surely it should be obvious that the academy must make its own judgment about the social value of the tasks it is called upon to perform. Even if the federal government wants war research or political stability studies or officer training, the professors and stu-dents of the university may decide that the government is *wrong* and that its desires should be resisted. If someone asks what right the professors and students have to question the will of the federal government, we can only reply, what right has the federal govern-ment to impose its will upon free men and women?

But there are material conditions of freedom, as a Marxist might say, and a university too heavily dependent upon federal grants will find itself unable to take a stand against programs and directions of development which it believes to be wrong. It is honorable for the workers in a government agency to accept the policy direction of Congress and the President. They exist to effect the will of the people, which expresses itself through its elected representatives. But it is *dishonorable* for a university to become a government agency by forfeiting the active exercise of its power of independent evaluation.

So many of the hopes and fears of the American people [Kerr writes] are now related to our educational system and particularly to our universities—the hope for longer life, for getting into outer space, for a higher standard of living; our fears of Russian or Chinese supremacy, of the bomb and annihilation, of individual loss of purpose in the changing world. For all these reasons and others, the university has become a prime instrument of national purpose [p. 87].

Kerr's voice is the voice of praise, but his words are an unwitting indictment of the modern university.

So we come to our last criticism of the multiversity. If it is an *instrument* of national purpose, then it cannot be a *critic* of national purpose, for an instrument is a means, not an evaluator of ends. In America today the power of the federal government has grown so great that there is almost no independent center of activity with the authority to challenge its policies. Within the broad consensus of practical politics there are countless disagreements and conflicts of belief or interest, but when the very premises of that consensus are wrong, who is to combat them? The great universities stand alone as institutions rich enough, powerful enough, possessed of sufficient moral and intellectual authority to cry Nay, Nay, when every other voice says Yea, Yea. There is no better example of this "power of negation," as the Hegelians might say, than the case of the Vietnam Teach-ins. Without overestimating their role in the great shift of opinion which eventually brought Johnson down and drove the government to the peace table, I think it is fair to say that the public debates staged by dissenting professors and students were the turning point in the history of America's involvement in Vietnam.

Clark Kerr's vision of the university of social service poses a great choice to those of us who care about the future of the academy. Shall the university accept the symbiotic interactions with government which are now offered? Shall it devote its resources to the satisfaction of those social desires which make themselves felt as effective demands? Or shall it remain institutionally aloof and counterpose itself to the momentum of government, foundation, and industry? It won't do to strike for a middle course, thinking that we can accept the government's money and be admitted to the council chambers while yet remaining free to dissent. Perhaps we might persuade ourselves that such a course was honorable, but I fear we would soon find it in practice impossible. The federal government is not likely to underwrite a foreign service officers' training program with the understanding that the candidates will in their seminars explore the imperialist foundation of American foreign policy. Nor is the government likely to show much patience for a federally supported laboratory which diverts its grant money to the development and publication of techniques for guerrilla insurgency against American forces.*

It comes down to this: at the present time in the United States, is there a greater social need for full-scale integration of the resources and activities of the universities into existing domestic and foreign programs, or for a sustained critique of those programs from an independent position of authority and influence? My own belief is that we need critique, not cooperation, and I therefore reject the model of the multiversity as an ideal for the modern university.

* I have no doubt that somewhere in the United States today a team of scientists is engaged in just such a study, for the purpose of alerting the United States military to the weaponry its forces will face in the 1970's. I trust the reader can see the difference between such a study and the sort of "anti-American" research I have in mind. The flexibility of the American government in the study of means is exceeded only by its rigidity in the pursuit of its agreed ends. What troubles me is the gradual extinction in the university of any spark of resistance to those ends.

CHAPTER FOUR

The University as an Assembly Line
for Establishment Man

We turn finally to an anti-model of the university, in terms of which contemporary student radicals mount their assault on university education in America. When the current movement of student protest got under way roughly five years ago, the original attacks were directed at specific conditions or policies which were felt to be immoral or inconsistent with a good education. In some universities, students renewed the old attack on Reserve Officer Training programs; in others, they protested the recruiting activities of corporations or government agencies with obvious military connections. Sometimes, as at Berkeley, students aimed their fire at teaching and staffing policies which produced large, impersonal classes and a minimum of student-teacher contact. But wherever the protests appeared, the targets were particular in nature. The unexpressed implication was that the university as a social institution was itself sound; the evils were not intrinsic to the institution but were *abuses* of it. Even in the Columbia affair, coming rather late in the development of events, the rebellious students stuck very closely to a set of six demands, each of which was concerned with a specific university action or policy.

As the several campus protests have grown into a movement, however, students have progressively generalized their criticism into something like a theory of what is wrong with higher education in America. Gradually a model of the university emerges and crystallizes, laying bare the connections between its underlying structure and the variety of visible evils which manifest themselves here and there.*

* The movement from particular, disconnected complaints against abuses of the existing institutions to a coherent, general critique of the institution itself

43

In its fully developed form, the radical critique of the American university consists of three elements—or, as philosophers like to say, three moments. These are: a thoroughgoing criticism of the content and organization of education within the university; an account of the relation of the university as an institution to the other major institutions of our society, in particular to the government, to industry, and to the military; and a theory about how the first is causally related to the second.* I shall do my best to rehearse the critique as forcefully as I can. First, however, it might be helpful to bring into the open and debunk once for all a rather silly notion of the university which plays a large role in the rhetoric, if not in the theorizing, of radical students these days.

The theory, which we might call a vulgar Marxist heresy, runs something like this: the university in capitalist society is [like a] corporation, run by administrators and trustees (and faculty—the theory is confused about their role) in the interest of the institution and of the capitalists, many of whom are to be found in administrative positions. The students are an exploited and down-trodden proletariat, maltreated and manipulated by their bosses. Liberation will come through solidarity, organization, and the permanent overthrow of the university power structure by an alliance of students together with those junior faculty who choose to throw in with the progressive class of students.

---

is of course a familiar pattern. It is characteristic of "anti-ideological" liberals to remain fixated at the first stage, justifying their failure to progress beyond spot criticism and piecemeal reform as "pragmatic" or "hard-nosed." The ideological result is a covert rationalization of existing institutions, for no evil is ever perceived as *intrinsic* to the institutions rather than a mere *abuse* of it. For a more systematic discussion of this subject, see my *Poverty of Liberalism*, Chapter Three, "Power." See also Herbert Marcuse's discussion of the repressive effects of behavioral social science in *One-Dimensional Man* (Boston: Beacon Press, 1964). The source of these several discussions is Marx's theory of class-consciouness.

* I don't know whether any student radicals have formulated their theory quite this coherently and systematically. I have had trouble finding an SDS publication, for example, in which the argument is laid down clearly enough to permit a lengthy quotation and analysis. Nevertheless, I shall stand by my reconstruction as capturing the essential structure of the thing if not all of its variety of detail.

There are three reasons, I think, why this grotesque misrepresentation of the character of a university appeals so viscerally to a number of rebellious students. First of all, it is a readymade rhetoric, complete with slogans, emotional associations, rallying cries, and symbols—the red flag of communism, the black flag of anarchism, "All power to the Soviets," "communes," and so forth. This is a noble revolutionary legacy, nicely calculated to drive sober, middle-aged liberal administrators wild. At Columbia, émigré professors who should have known better lost all sense of reality and panicked, freely predicting another major reign of terror if the "young hoodlums" were not immediately and forcefully put down.

Secondly, the fantasy that the students are the proletariat rebelling against their capitalist exploiters carries with it the comfortable corollary that they are riding the wave of the future. As the Bolsheviks studied the French Revolution and adjusted their expectations accordingly, so a number of radical students enjoy the thought that they are the eighty-one in the Sierra Maestra, or the spearhead of an American Long March.

Finally, of course, students find it morally comforting to identify themselves as a suffering proletariat, because in their souls there echoes the old Judeo-Christian belief that suffering cleanses and ennobles. At all costs, some students must see themselves as victims, sufferers, the exploited, the wretched of the university community. It is as though they had once read Socrates' injunction, "It is better to suffer injustice than to commit injustice," and misremembered it as, "It is better to suffer injustice than *not* to suffer injustice"!

The bits and pieces of working-class movement rhetoric appear in calls for a student "strike," or for "student solidarity," or in the view of the university as composed of classes with conflicting class interests. Actually, though, the rhetoric is all wrong. If one were to give a quasi-Marxist analysis of the university, it would look something like this:

The university is like a capitalist firm. The trustees are the board of directors and the administration is the management. The workers are not the students, but the *faculty*. The firm manufactures a line of consumer goods, namely, its various *degrees*. The students, of course, are the *consumers*. They buy the product put out by the firm. There is a genuine conflict of class interests between the management and the workers—i.e., between the administration and the faculty. As usual, the workers want higher wages, shorter hours, better working conditions, fringe benefits, and job security. When the supply of labor far exceeds the demand, then working conditions and wages are poor. For some time now, however, higher education has been undergoing very rapid growth. Like all growth industries with a high technological component and skilled labor force (such as petrochemicals or electronics), higher education experiences high wages, good working conditions, and a very mobile labor force, with a good deal of intra-industry raiding.

In the industry as a whole, there is a surplus of supply over demand (i.e., empty places in freshman classes each Fall), but the quality of the product varies enormously from firm to firm, and there is a perpetual shortage of the most sought-after degrees. This quite naturally drives up the price, particularly since the quality firms maintain an artificially short supply through oligopolistic techniques of market control. Oddly enough, the industry's leading firms do not exact the high market price for their product in *dollars*. In fact, they sell their degrees at a considerable dollar loss. But they *do* exact an extremely high price from their customers in the form of certain behavior patterns and performances which they make prerequisites for the sale of the degree. By and large, those customers who pay the price for the scarce quality degrees get value for their money and effort. Their earning power and status opportunities increase quite satisfactorily. Since this fact is well known, an ever-larger pool of potential customers is formed and competition for the scarce products is fierce. Under these labor and market conditions, the workers (i.e., faculty) have considerable bargaining power, and they therefore do quite well even without collective bargaining. Were they to threaten to strike a single large firm (university), they could easily bring it to its knees. The customers (students), on the other hand, cannot effectively employ the traditional consumers' weapon of a boycott (*not* a "strike"). There are too many potential customers ready to take their places, should they try.

This little parody is not entirely wide of the mark. In particular, the bit about universities demanding behavior rather than money from their "customers" strikes close to home, and one might sum up a good deal of recent student discontent by saying that more and more consumers of higher education are deciding that the product is not worth the nonmonetary price. But the gap between parody and reality is still enormous, and there is much to be learned from that fact. The moral relationships among capitalist, worker, and consumer are simply nothing like those among administrators, faculty, and students. Different criteria of value guide choices and action on all sides, different norms of acceptable behavior operate, different criteria of success and failure are invoked by each community in allocating the nonmaterial rewards of status and approbation. The Rolls-Royce dealer with six cars and forty rich customers would simply turn his back on a purchaser who complained about the style of the Rolls. If you don't like it, don't buy it, he would say, and invite the next customer into his office. But no Ivy League dean, even in a fit of total exasperation, would summarily expel rebellious students on the grounds that plenty of other young men with high College Board scores were waiting to be admitted. Much of the frustration which students suffer in their confrontations derives from their knowledge that it is the forbearance of faculty and dean, not their own power, which keeps them from being thrown out on the spot. They are forced to rely on the fact that the university is precisely *not* a capitalist firm merely out to make a profit, but rather is an educational institution dedicated—for better or worse—to *their* intellectual development.

But attractive though the fantasy of the suffering proletariat may be, it plays no important part in the serious critique of the university on which the radical students base their attacks. Let us turn therefore to the three-stage radical analysis of what is wrong with American colleges and universities.

The starting point of the critique is a subjective fact—a feeling, not an axiom or a theory. Large numbers of the brightest, most enthusiastic, curious, eager, academically turned-on students in America are thoroughly dissatisfied with the education they are offered in universities today. The students most profoundly disturbed are precisely those who might be expected to enjoy college the most. They are the college-oriented, the academic achievers, the very students to whom the curriculum and university life are tailored in the best schools. It is worth reflecting for a moment on the significance of this basic fact, because it frequently gets lost in the confusion and emotion of demonstrations and confrontations. The first principle of institutional diagnostics is that something is wrong when those best suited to the life of the institution rebel most violently against it. If the secular at heart drift away from Rome, the Church can comfort itself that not all are called to the service of God; but when the priests rebel, then it is almost certainly the Church itself which is at fault. So too, professors need not be unsettled by the defection of students who are obviously unsuited for the activities of the academy. But the rebels today are the best students, not the worst. And that can only mean trouble in the university itself.

When I say "the best students," I do not mean merely the "A" students, although the universal experience is that the rebels number in their ranks some of the most successful students by grading standards. I mean those young men and women whose alert and probing minds mark them as natural participants in the life of the mind.

The discontent is at first vague, imprecise, unarticulated, as one might expect. Students who have fought a vicious battle to win admission to a top school find that the experience there falls short of their expectation. They rebel against regulations for which they see no reason. They struggle to fight free of educational restrictions and requirements which stifle rather than stimulate their interest. They see no point in the endless testing and grading to which so much of the genuinely educational activity of the campus is subordinated. They grow impatient with their professors' calm assurance that the facts and techniques they master now will prove valuable to them later on. Their education, they protest, is not *relevant*, by which they mean that it speaks neither to their needs nor to the needs of the world. It is *specialized*, they say, or *professional*—meaning mostly that it seems dull and pointless.

At the same time, the students find themselves part of an academic community which has intimate relations with the larger world of American society. It is *their* community; they identify with it immediately and completely. But it does things they detest, and it is run by men with whom they feel no bond of sympathy or understanding. It contracts with the government for war research; it confers honorary degrees on industrial tycoons and puts slumlords on its boards of governors; it runs officer-training programs, welcomes defense industry firms as recruiters, and establishes professional schools to train future State Department officials.

Now one might expect that a student who disapproved of these activities would simply turn his back on the university, or at least close his heart to it. Not at all. The university is his world, his turf, his home. Nothing is more striking than the speed with which the new student identifies the university as *his university*, so that his criticisms come from the inside rather than the outside. Senior professors with thirty years of service behind them may deprecate the rebels as outsiders, newcomers who have yet to earn the right to criticize the institution; but to the rebels themselves, the newest registrant is as completely a part of the community as the oldest emeritus professor. Indeed, that is the principal reason for the bitterness of the attacks, which resemble family feuds rather than political conflicts.

So strong is their identification with the university that although the rebels will criticize it, condemn it, revile it, obstruct it, even— God forbid—burn it down, the one thing they will not do is simply turn their backs on it and walk away. They are truly the children of the university, and so it is not surprising that their ultimate act of rejection is to step outside the walls of the academy and found their own Free University in its shadow. All the essentials of a university can be found there—teachers, students, courses, reading lists. Only the titles are different: revolutionary drama, rather than Shakespeare; a history of revolutions rather than a history of France; guerrilla tactics rather than a statistical approach to voting behavior. But university curricula are flexible, and there is hardly a course in a Free University which could not be comfortably accommodated in the establishment next door.

When the radical students try to put their frustration and discontent together in a coherent form, their critique goes something like this: the university is indeed like an industrial firm in capitalist society, but its product is not a degree, as in our little parody, nor are students the customers of the firm. The product of the university, to alter a famous description by an older liberal critic, is the *Establishment Man*. The customers for this product are the corporations, government agencies, foundations, military services, *and universities* whose destructive, repressive, antisocial activities demand an ever-larger supply of loyal and unquestioning workers. The students are the raw material from which the university fashions its product. Strictly speaking, the universities are only the final stage in a productive process which begins in elementary schools, or even prior to that in the home. The Establishment Man is a highly productive worker, but he is very expensive to produce. Consequently, the firms who purchase him must pay a high price, in taxes and "voluntary" contributions, to the colleges and universities of America. Viewed in isolation, a university may seem to be a nonprofit organization supported by charitable donations; but seen as part of the total advanced industrial economy, the university proves to be as profitable as an executive training program, a union apprentice system, or indeed any intermediate step in production through which raw materials must pass before becoming salable in the market place.

Viewed as an exercise in labor training and discipline, the activity of the university is seen to pose very complex and tricky problems, whose solution calls for great skill and imagination on the part of faculty and administration. Technologically advanced capitalism requires a large number of workers who combine technical skill with a high level of imagination, inventiveness, and individual initiative. The system demands growth, which in turn rests on innovation both technical and administrative. Now, men cannot be coerced or bribed into the sorts of creative activity necessary for continued economic growth. The motivation must be internal, and it must be something more than mere greed or acquisitiveness. When Robert McNamara reorganized the command structure of the Ford Motor Company, he was driven by pride, by the excitement of putting into practice the theories he had taught at Harvard Business School, by a desire to put his stamp on a huge industrial bureaucracy. The same motives operated in him as Secretary of Defense, during which time there was no question of his private gain.

Unfortunately (so the radical critique continues), men who are encouraged to think and act creatively may very well begin to question the values of the system for which they are being prepared. Their doubts may extend beyond the merits of wealth and status to the very foundation stone of the system—production for profit rather than for use. They may become first critics, and then active opponents, of capitalism at home and imperialism abroad. But it will not do to guard against this danger by stifling originality and initiative, for thereby one stifles profits as well. Some way must be found to provoke an outpouring of creative energy in profitable directions, while misdirecting the attention of productive Establishment Men from the glaring evils and injustices of the social and economic system they are about to enter. This complex double task, the radicals argue, is precisely the concealed goal of the education in America's colleges and universities.

It works like this: starting initially in elementary school, bright students are presented with challenging and interesting materials in the natural sciences and humanities. At the same time, they are made vividly aware of the severe competition for desirable slots at the higher levels. Before they are old enough to question the value of the prizes they compete for, students are launched on a desperate race for college, for graduate school, and beyond. Everywhere they turn—to their families, to friends, books, television, movies—they see the rewards of success in the race they are running. Society really *does* pay off on success. Those who win the race are wealthy, famous, honored; they have leisure, luxury, and exciting opportunities for new experiences. What is more, the successful ones even get to tackle the really challenging new tasks.

It is the "A" students, not the "C" students, who perform heart transplants, argue landmark cases before the Supreme Court, advise Presidents, and take control of giant corporations.

The anxious students, oppressed by the competition for success, suffer an intellectual block which makes them unable to see the evils of the system they are struggling to enter. The undergraduate years, which might well provide a brief, quiet moment for reflection, are infected by the competition for graduate and professional schools.

But even in so repressive a society, there are voices which cry a warning, critics who question the very basis of the system rather than merely quibbling about its details. These voices are a threat to the system, for like the boy who insisted that the emperor had no clothes on, they pierce the hypocrisy and point to the evils which lie before our very eyes.

To meet this challenge, the proprietors of the system—the educators—have devised a masterstroke, a brilliant device for emasculating and domesticating the critics. Rather than argue against them, which would elevate their importance, or censor them, which would confer all the appeal of martyrdom upon them, the intellectual establishment welcomes the critics into the academy and puts their books on the required reading list! Mastering the condemnations of the system becomes one of the conditions of success in the system.

The academic establishment defends itself against these charges by insisting that it takes no stand on the issues of war or peace, capitalism or socialism. As a setting for inquiry and debate, it remains strictly value neutral. Perhaps so, the radicals reply, so far as the *content* of university education is concerned; there is no ban in the academy on the works of Marx, Lenin, Mao, or Che Guevara. But the *form* of the education defeats content, no matter how radical. Theory is divorced from practice, students grub for grades in courses on revolution as eagerly as in courses on organic chemistry or the philosophy of the Enlightenment. Competition sets students against one another even in courses devoted to the study of cooperation and community. And always the system grinds on relentlessly, taking in lively, eager boys and girls and spewing forth precision-tooled Establishment Men. Can McGeorge Bundy ever have been a child?

The false consciousness of the educational process—the anxious emphasis on artificial goals, the stifling of genuine creativity and critical intelligence, the concealment of the real purposes of the institution—merely mirrors the false consciousness in the society as a whole. Production for profit rather than use has its analogue in scholarship for publication rather than for wisdom. The continued illusion of harmony between labor and management is echoed in the pretense that students and faculty have a common interest. And just as the exclusion of the poor and the Black from the most advantageous jobs is rationalized by their lack of appropriate training, so the exclusion of their children from the best universities is rationalized by appeal to high school grades and aptitude scores. To be sure, there is tokenism in the university as in industry; but so long as corporations produce for profit and universities educate for safe performance rather than for radical self-fulfillment, both institutions will comfortably discover that the poor and the Black simply do not measure up.

Thus we have a critique of the university and a critique of society, but is there a causal link or merely a striking parallel between the two? How does the university come to reflect so perfectly the values of the society? (Or should we say, with certain American sociologists of an idealist persuasion, that the institutions of the society reflect the values of the university?)

The answer is the third and connecting link in the chain of radical argument. The needs, values, and hypocrisies of the larger society are inflicted upon the university through the financing procedure of university education and through the intimidation of the higher university administration. So long as the lion's share of the money for universities comes from industry, foundations, and state and federal governments, society at large can effectively dictate the form and content of the education within the academy. Sometimes, of course, the dictation is direct and rather brutal, particularly in state universities run by conservative state legislatures. But usually the pressures are subtle and indirect—carrots rather than sticks. We have already looked at the ways in which the professions impose standards on professional schools. In much the same way, the desires of corporations reflect back into undergraduate programs from which they intend to draw their junior executives.

Sometimes, the pressures are so indirect as to disappear from sight. For example, in response to Soviet space successes, a National Defense Education Act was passed, creating graduate fellowships and providing money to strengthen areas of university activity which the Congress deems valuable to America's military ambitions. The heavyhanded loyalty oath and affidavit requirements of the NDEA fellowships have received a great deal of publicity, but the real coercive effect of NDEA on graduate education has little to do with such know-nothing excrescences. Even if they were eliminated, the major pressure would remain. The mechanism is this: the government makes available to universities much-needed fellowship money. The universities respond by accepting the money *and applying the funds thus freed to other pressing needs* (such as faculty salaries). Now, the NDEA grants run for a term of three years. This places an enormous pressure on students to complete their graduate work quickly, because their university, having allocated its funds, is apt not to have further scholarship aid available when those three years are up. Typically, a graduate student on an NDEA grant will study for three years and then teach as an assistant for several years while trying to complete his dissertation. But if students are pressured to finish quickly, then the content of the graduate program must be adjusted so that the average good student can master it in the allotted time. Thus, by a chain of consequences, the government's laudable allocation of money to graduate fellowships ends by squeezing *all* graduate study into a lockstep which bears no intrinsic relation whatever to the logic of each individual discipline.

Over and above the direct and indirect financial pressures which bear upon the university, the values of the society are guaranteed a place in the academy by the way in which the university is ruled. Representatives of the military-government-industrial establishment sit on the governing boards of universities and appoint their chief executive officers. Even though university presidents are frequently former professors, they are selected by nonprofessors who quite naturally co-opt into the ranks of the administration only those whose attitudes are congenial to the establishment. Eventually, of course, the combination of these various internal and external pressures produces a class of professors who have quite thoroughly internalized the false and hypocritical standards of the system. Hence even a university reorganization which places power in the hands of the faculty will not have a noticeable effect on the life of the institution. Indeed, cries of faculty power serve the same ideological function as did nineteenth-century reformist calls for extension of the suffrage. The evil inheres in the system itself, and nothing short of a radical separation of the university from society, or even a reorganization of society itself, can replace false values with true values and education for repression with education for liberation.

What shall we say of this attack on American higher education? It should be obvious, from the passion with which I expound it, that there is much in it which I consider true and important. Certification, ranking, and professional criteria of success *do* intrude on the educational life of the university, and their effect is almost always destructive. Young men and women are required, at precisely the wrong time in their lives, to behave either like little children or like middle-aged careerists. Every attempt at imagination, flexibility, and experiment—and there are many superb attempts— must struggle against the extraneous and irrelevant demands of the system for grades, prerequisites, certificates of "good standing." It is as though the act of love were governed by civil service regulations. In Part Two, I will discuss the differences between the legitimate educational activity of *criticism* and the irrelevant activities of ranking and certification. Later, I will suggest a way in which undergraduate education might be at least partially insulated from career pressures and demands. I am also in sympathy with the radical criticism of American society at large, although neither I nor the other critics can offer adequately reasoned proposals for systematic change. Finally, I take it as too obvious to dispute that the university experiences great pressures and manifold influences from the corporate, eleemosynary, military, and governmental worlds; considering American higher education as a whole, much of what happens in universities is explainable only in terms of the operations of such outside forces.

Nevertheless, the radical critique of the university is wrong on several important counts. To begin with, despite the pressures and constraints of contemporary higher education, it seems to me clearly the case that university life is *liberating* for most students, and that the liberation occurs *because* of what the university is rather than *in spite of* what it is. To repeat—and I fear that many repetitions will be necessary—I am *not* suggesting that American universities are satisfactory as they stand, or that the only changes needed are marginal adjustments. I am only claiming that *even now*, a great many colleges and universities are much freer, much more conducive to serious questioning and open debate, much more committed to human values, than any other major institution in the United States. Their effect is to promote in students a reexamination of the unquestioned religious, moral, social, economic, and political dogmas by which men customarily live. Indeed, one of the causes of student rebellion is the contradiction between their newly awakened awareness and the old social constraints and demands which still bear down upon them. Once an undergraduate sees how devoid of intellectual importance his grades really are, it is trebly painful to be forced still to worry about them and compete for them.

I am equally in disagreement with the radicals' view of the relation of the university to American society. American universities today, despite their defense contracts and ROTC programs, their businessman trustees and Establishment presidents, are the only major viable institutional centers of opposition to the dominant values and policies of the society. The churches are weak, the unions have long since made their peace with the established order, the poor and the Black are as yet not organized, and little can be expected from the corporate world or the agricultural sector. It is in universities that opposition to the Vietnamese war started and flourished. There, if anywhere, new and deeper attacks on the evils of American society will be mounted. *Here again, the opposition role of the university flows from its very nature as a center of free inquiry.* Against all the pressures from the larger society, colleges and universities in the United States have for half a century been in the van of progressive social reform and social criticism.

I am enough of an old-fashioned Marxist to believe that societies cannot, by an effort of will or outburst of utopian fervor, leap over major steps in social progress. If the universities are at the head of such progress, then anything which strengthens them is to the good, and anything which weakens them can only have a reactionary effect. To be sure, the next possible stage of social development may still fall far short of our dream of the good society, but no twist of Hegelian Dialectic will persuade me that a society progresses by destroying its most progressive institution. Many students now feel so great a revulsion against contemporary America that they cannot mobilize their emotional energies for anything less than a total, revolutionary transformation of society. I sympathize with them. Their condition is in no way dishonorable, and if I were younger, less settled in a career, and less entangled in the intense personal relationships of marriage and parenthood, I think I might share their feelings entirely. But the fact remains that only next steps are ever possible; final steps can never be taken. So those of us who can still sustain a concern for the partial amelioration of social evils must rely upon the actual institutions which offer us the most assistance. In America today, the university clearly heads that list.

PART TWO

Partisan Thoughts About Some
Educational Controversies

CHAPTER ONE

A Discourse on Grading

For most American students, the dominant educational fact for the first eighteen years of schooling—if they last that long—is the *Grade*. From those first simple report cards which the first-grader carries home, through the quiz grades, paper grades, test grades, aptitude scores, and college boards, to the course grades, honors thesis grades, and Law School Aps or Graduate Record scores, the American student lives, breathes, grows, and defines himself in a world of grades. To some, grades are merely a harassment; to others, they are a mild incentive. But in many young people, the brightest and most promising among them, a fixation on grades develops. Rather like misers, who begin by craving wealth and end by craving its symbol, these students develop a pathological anxiety over the grades themselves, quite independently of their usefulness or significance. The fetishism of commodities gives way to a fetishism of marks, and as the pathological consumer will window-shop even when he has no money, merely to be near commodities and draw comfort from them, so the grade lover (or "achievement-oriented" student, as it is fashionable to call him) soothes himself with recollections of near-perfect test scores and straight-A semesters, "He had 800's on his College Boards!" expresses the same intensity of libidinal cathexis as do the numbers "38–24–38" in a somewhat different context. Despite the concentration of attention on the activity of grading, the subject is terribly confused. Even teachers, for whom grading is one of the principal activities of their professional life, frequently have very little idea why they give grades at all and what the conditions would be under which they could dispense with grading.

There are three different activities which commonly go under the name of "grading." Before we can determine the role of grading in the ideal university, we must sort out the several kinds of grading and consider their relationship to the process of education. The three species of grading are *criticism, evaluation,* and *ranking.*

Criticism is the analysis of a product or performance for the purpose of identifying and correcting its faults or reinforcing its excellences. Thus a teacher will correct a spelling error or incorrect sentence construction, show a student where he has gone wrong in a geometry proof, or pronounce correctly the French phrase which the pupil has garbled. So too, at a more advanced level, a professor will point out an incoherence in the development of an argument, or call attention to significant data which have been ignored. At the elementary level of spelling and syntax (which even the writers of doctoral dissertations must attend to, alas), there is not a great deal of disagreement over what is correct and what is not. When more complex matters of style, argument, and evidence are at stake, however, criticism becomes inextricably bound up with intellectual norms which themselves may be matters of dispute. A teacher who criticizes a student's work for concentrating upon unimportant issues, or for using terms which are unclear, or for ignoring certain kinds of evidence, inevitably expresses his own normative commitments. Hence, at the most advanced levels of education, both teacher and student must be aware of the possibility that they simply are wrong for one another and might better discontinue their relationship.

Evaluation is the measuring of a product or performance against an independent and objective standard of excellence. It issues characteristically in some sort of *grade* which expresses the teacher's judgment of the absolute merit of the student's performance. For example, a teacher may have some idea in mind of what constitutes an acceptable performance in arithmetic. Any student who surpasses that level receives a pass-grade; the others are failed.

Sometimes the teacher will measure performance against a linear scale, permitting grades of "excellent, good, pass, and fail," or "A, B, C, D, and F," or even—where fine discrimination among performances are possible—a continuous range of grades from zero to one hundred.

The whole subject of scales of measurement is rather more complicated than it appears on the surface. It is quite possible for a grading system to discriminate between unacceptable and acceptable performances, and yet fail to provide a linear scale of grades along which the various performances can be located. Thus, a connoisseur of violin playing may feel quite confident in judging some performances as excellent and others not, without however having any way of deciding among excellent performances by Heifetz, Milstein, and Oistrakh. The problem is not that they play "equally well," but that beyond a certain level of technical skill and interpretative finesse a choice among them becomes a matter of taste. *But*—and this is a very important point not often appreciated by students—the difference between a great violinist and a bad fiddler *is* a matter of objective evaluation, even though only taste can guide us in choosing among great violinists. Doctoral candidates in philosophy, for example, frequently imagine that faculty disagreements over dissertations stem from doctrinal differences which only taste can resolve; whereas in fact the dispute is usually over whether the dissertation meets those minimal standards on which partisans of every ideology can agree.

Some sort of evaluative standard is usually implicit in acts of criticism, although there is no necessary connection between the two. When Pablo Casals conducts a master class in the cello, he may of course merely correct wrong fingerings or phrasings and suggest differences in interpretation, but he is likely as well to say "that was very good" after a particularly lovely bit of playing. This suggests that he has in mind a conception of the *right* way to play the piece, against which he measures the performances of his pupils.

In many intellectual activities, reality itself provides at least a partial scale of objective evaluation. If the historian seeks to discover what happened in some past time, then the primary measure of his success is the truth of what he asserts, not its wit or charm or the felicity of his expression. The most delightful false account is bad history; its literary worth cannot make up for gross errors of fact, as Thomas Carlyle's famous work on the French Revolution shows. But truth is not enough either in history or in the sciences. As someone once said of sociology, the problem is not to say something true, but to say something important. Generally speaking, one can get very wide agreement in the arts and sciences about what constitutes a *bad* performance, but very little agreement on the criteria of *good* or *excellent* performances. Even in the professions, this generalization seems to hold. Doctors will agree that X is a bad doctor, and lawyers that Y is an incompetent lawyer. But ask them who are the great doctors and lawyers, and opinions may vary as widely as the criteria of importance and significance to which the several practitioners owe their allegiance.

Where an objective linear scale of excellence is perceived by the evaluator, the choice of the grading system will be determined by two factors: the number of discrete levels of performance which can be distinguished with any certainty, and the needs of the institution in which the grading is done. The simplest system is pass-fail, or acceptable-unacceptable. To this may be added the grade of distinction; then the grades excellent and good; until finally we arrive at the familiar five-step grading systems used in many college and graduate courses: "A, B, C, D, and F."* The move to a numerical system involves no new assumptions about the process of grading, and the widespread suspicion of numerical grades on the part of those who are quite content with "A"s and "B"s is a mere superstition. The virtue of numbers, of course, is that they can be aggregated and averaged, making possible a comparative ranking of students who have been evaluated in a number of performances.

Ranking is the grading activity which produces the greatest anxiety and provokes the most opposition. It is a relative comparison of the performances of a number of students, for the purpose of

* Harvard, with admirable consistency, refuses to be beguiled by the accident that "F" is the initial letter of "fail." It uses a grading system of "A, B, C, D, and E."

determining a linear ordering of comparative excellence. The simplest ranking is the sort which mathematicians call "ordinal"—that is to say, *best, second best, third best,* and so on down to *worst.* Such a ranking says nothing about *how much* better one student is than another. In a class of twenty students, the difference between the first and the last may be so small that it taxes the ability of the teacher to distinguish among their performances. Sometimes the difference is enormous, a fact which creates very great teaching problems. My own experience is that in the classes I have taught at Harvard, Chicago, Wellesley, and Columbia, there is a huge gap in excellence of performance between the "A" students and the "B" students, a marginal gap between the low "B" and high "C" students, and another very large gap between the solid "C" students and those who are marginal or actually failing. The difference between the best and the worst is likely to be so great that calling them all students in the same course is more an act of faith than a statement of fact. My criticisms of the work of the best deal with nuances of style and subtleties of argumentation. Those at the other end of the scale are still struggling to master the syntactical structure of English sufficiently to make elementary logical distinctions.

The difference between evaluation and ranking is captured in that anxious question so often on the lips of students, "Is this course graded on a curve?" Evaluation establishes a relationship between each student and an objective scale of measurement. Since in general the performances of students do not affect one another, it is perfectly possible for every student in a class to rank high on the scale, or for every student to fail. Some teachers however set the grade levels only *after* the students have been evaluated, so that a certain distribution of grades is guaranteed. Typically, they want a small number of failing grades and distinctions and a large number of low and high passes. The resulting distribution can be plotted on a graph in a familiar bell shape known as "the curve." Grading on a curve assures that the class will be sorted out along a scale of relative excellence, but of course it provides no clue to the level of performance signified by a particular grade. When I was a freshman, I took an extremely difficult physics course intended for prospective concentrators. The very best students in the class regularly scored more than 100 on examinations (there were bonus questions). The worst had negative grades (one was penalized so many points for each mistake). The mean was roughly 40. When the final grades were computed, my 38 earned me a "C+," but after looking over the distribution of grades the professor decided that there were not enough honor grades—the "curve was lowered," and I got my "B−." So it is that I can honestly say I did honor work in physics in college!

Criticism, evaluation, and ranking serve three entirely distinct functions in the process and institutions of education. *Criticism* lies at the very heart of education. To learn is to submit oneself to the discipline of a standard, *even if the standard is self-created and self-imposed.* The mathematician submits himself to standards of consistency and simplicity, the scientist to the standards of truth and explanatory power. The social scientist measures his work by its relevance to human concerns as well as by the scientist's standard of truth. The artist strives for beauty. The only way to become a mathematician, a physicist, a historian, or a poet is to put one's whole self into each attempt and then submit the result to criticism. Painful as criticism is, even from those one loves best or respects most, there is no other way to learn.

The most dangerous heresy of pedagogy is the popular belief that subjective feeling is the criterion of success in education. Repelled by the perverse and sadistic view that "it only helps if it hurts," countless educational rebels have proclaimed the doctrine that what counts is how the performance *feels* to the student himself. If he "feels good" about his poem or his philosophical argument, then nothing else matters. Education must liberate the student's libidinal energies and shun the stultifying criticism which seeks to shape those energies in ways dictated by the teacher.

There is, of course, a truth hidden in this heresy. When education has been reduced to repression, and learning to rote, the spontaneous energies of the student may over a time be so dampened that some extreme therapy is needed to reevoke them. A totally free environment may be necessary, in which any response is welcomed, and expression cheered. But, sooner or later, criticism must reenter the process if the energies are to be focused effectively and the expression acquire style. Unfortunately, some students suffer a deadening education for so long that they lose the courage to sustain their spontaneity in the face of even the mildest criticism. At the first word of correction, they retreat into sullen obedience and produce mechanically the performances they think are wanted from them. I have seen such students among the ranks of the ablest undergraduates at our best colleges, and it all but tears my heart out. Ghetto schools are populated by them, if Jonathan Kozol, Herbert Kohl, and others are to be believed.

Evaluation, unlike criticism, is external to education properly so-called. Once a teacher has shown a student how he can state an argument more cogently, express an insight with greater felicity of phrasing, or muster evidence more persuasively for a conclusion, nothing is gained educationally by adding the words "good" or "bad." Where an objective standard of success is intrinsic to the activity, as in the case of a geometry proof which either is or is not valid, or a poem which is or is not a true sonnet, it is of course educationally valuable for the teacher to tell the student whether the standard has been met. But such additions to the act of criticism fall far short of what is usually called "giving a grade."

The true rationale of evaluation is not educational but professional. When a candidate seeks admission to a profession on the basis of some performance, the judges must ascertain whether he has *qualified*. For prospective professors, lawyers, or doctors, "pass" means admission to the profession with the legal right to practice and make a living thereby; "fail" means exclusion, and if second chances have been exhausted, the necessity of looking for some other career.

Since the first, or bachelor's, degree is not in itself a qualifying degree for any profession, it would seem that colleges could dispense with the practice of grading their preprofessional undergraduates. As far as any educational considerations are concerned, this is perfectly true. But for a long time now, the professional schools and programs have burdened undergraduate education with a major part of their admissions problem. By requiring a bachelor's degree as a prerequisite for work toward "higher" degrees, the professional schools force the colleges to take on a grading task which is irrelevant to education and sometimes positively harmful. The college becomes obsessed with ensuring that students "satisfy the requirements for the degree," independently of whether or not they are fruitfully involved in the educational life of the community. Imagine two students in Columbia College. John is deeply committed to the study of American history, but he "fails" a number of courses in mathematics, languages, and literature. After making every allowance that a wise and generous administrator can permit himself, the Dean reluctantly informs John that he may not continue his education at Columbia. No one denies that he has been fruitfully engaged in his historical studies, but after all, a student who fails most of his courses cannot be permitted to keep enrolling for more work! William, by contrast, is a thoroughly uninspired student who maintains himself in good academic standing by distributing his energies prudently, if dispassionately, among his several courses. No professor or fellow student would for a moment pretend that William has ever had a genuine educational experience at Columbia, but in due course he is awarded the Bachelor of Arts degree and welcomed to the company of Columbia alumni. Everything in the organization and conduct of Columbia College (or virtually any other American liberal arts college) conspires to persuade John that he is a failure and William that he is a success. And yet the sole justification for such a lamentable state of affairs is the necessity of ensuring that "Columbia graduates" are qualified for whatever further educational or professional endeavors they may undertake. Would anyone deny that a genuine, lasting, disciplined commitment to a single field of inquiry results in a more successful education than a continuous but impersonal fulfillment of an appropriate set of degree requirements? And yet, how many professors and deans—or students, for that matter—can be found who will argue for giving John a degree as well as William?

Ranking, as distinguished from evaluation and criticism, performs a function which is neither professional nor educational, but merely—in the broad sense—economic. The purpose of comparative ranking is to facilitate the fair allocation of scarce resources and utilities. Education is not in itself a scarce commodity (though opportunities for education may very well be). The Ideas, as Plato would have put it, can be embodied in any number of examples; the Pythagorean theorem does not flicker and grow dim as more and more minds embrace it. So far as the development of disciplined intelligence is concerned, it hardly matters who is first, second, or third. Nor does professional qualification intrinsically demand a ranking of the successful candidates. There are no national quotas of doctors or lawyers or architects;* qualification requires only a simple pass or fail, in or out.

Ranking only becomes necessary when more people want something than the available supply can satisfy. It is not admission to college which demands a ranking of high school graduates—for each Fall there are more places in freshman classes across the land than qualified students to fill them—but admission to the small number of highly *desired* colleges.** Similarly, if there were scholarships for all who needed them, no elaborate system of nationwide tests would be necessary; but there is a shortage of money, so naturally the applicants must be *ranked*.

It is really rather startling to reflect that the SOLE justification for all that frenzied, anxious test-taking and grade-grubbing which absorbs millions of American teenagers is the differential allocation of high school seniors to colleges in varying degrees of demand! No other intellectual, cultural, social, spiritual, psychological, or educational purpose is served by it. If places in colleges were assigned at random to all students meeting certain minimal standards of qualification, there would not be a single good reason for a secondary school student to worry about whether his grades placed him first in the nation or just barely above the cutoff point.

The same is true, of course, for college ranking and admission to the favored graduate and professional schools. Up to a point, as I

---

* Not officially, at any rate. I am not concerned here with the current attempts of the medical and some other professions to restrict artificially the numbers admitted to their ranks, in the interest of keeping incomes high.

** I use this awkward locution in order to leave open the question whether everything which is *desired* is also *desirable*. Needless to say, the two are not always identical.

have noted, professional schools use college grades as evidence of minimal qualification; but those schools with more applicants than places rely upon relative rankings, together with such ranking devices as objective tests and letters of recommendation, to establish an order of priority among the candidates. Here again, no other purpose is served by cumulative grade averages, class rank, and all the other devices for the making of efficient invidious comparisons among students.

It would be pleasant to think that the repeated ranking ceases on admission to a graduate or professional program, but of course that is not so. Beyond graduate school lies the world, and there again favored places must be assigned to top-ranking candidates. The choice residency, the junior partnership in Wall Street firms, the assistant professorship at the Ivy League university, all such places are for the best-qualified, not for the merely qualified. I think it is fair to say that the first title or degree conferred without differential ranking in the academic world is professor emeritus!

So ranking serves to apportion a scarce supply of *desired* places. Are those places also *desirable*, or is the endless competition a struggle for illusory rewards? I wish I could honestly say that the battle is a sham, but alas, the rewards are real enough for those few who make it to the top. The desired colleges really do offer a better education than those whose freshman classes are perpetually undermanned. The students are brighter, the faculty more exciting, the physical surroundings more pleasant, the cultural life richer. Harvard, Yale, Princeton, Columbia, Swarthmore, Amherst, and the rest are truly better schools. To be sure, a bright and eager student can find an exciting education at a hundred other schools across the country; but even those hundred are the best of the more than two thousand colleges and universities. As for graduate and professional schools, the difference between the favored and the forgotten is, if anything, even greater. There are three dozen American universities, at most, where one can study philosophy profitably. The student who does not win admission to one of those departments is probably better off reading philosophy on his own.

I need hardly elaborate on the differential distribution of rewards available to candidates who have actually entered into professional practice. An income of two hundred thousand dollars a year and the power that goes with a senior partnership in a Wall Street law firm bears little relationship to the lower-middle-class existence of the courthouse hack who battens on the machine bosses and picks up a living from defending clients accused of petty larceny. The victory may not be worth the battle, but there can be no question that in the American educational system today, the spoils belong to the victor.

It should be obvious that there is no easy way to disentangle education from the essentially extraneous processes of evaluation and ranking. So long as some colleges and professional schools really offer better educational opportunities and a competitive edge in the struggle for wealth, power, and status in American society, there will be more applicants than places at every stage in the educational system from kindergarten to graduate school. It is a bitter irony that the competition is merely intensified by the painstaking efforts of administrators to make the selection process more just.

The evil inheres in the scarcity of desired places and the dependence of social rewards on educational accomplishment, not in any particular system of grading. Nothing is to be gained, for example, by substituting written evaluations for numerical grades. Letters of recommendation degenerate into discursive rankings when many candidates seek few places. As with all of the most intractable social evils, this destructive competition is the product of a social *virtue*, namely, the effective implementation of the principle of equality of opportunity.

Later on, I shall suggest some ways in which evaluation and ranking might be at least partially separated from education itself, but there are no clever reforms or institutional tricks which will effect a total separation. Only a social revolution of the most far-reaching sort could free education from the twin curses of evaluation and ranking.

CHAPTER TWO

Three Myths of Education

A. THE MYTH OF VALUE NEUTRALITY

In the dialectic of charge, response, and confrontation which dominates the campus these days, one of the most familiar disputes revolves about the role of the university as supporter or opponent of government policy. Characteristically, the interchange proceeds something like this:

1. The university is engaged in a variety of extra-educational activities, such as contract research, the scheduling of job interviews, transmission of class standing to draft boards, and so forth. These activities accumulate haphazardly without deliberate university control and in the absence of a coherent policy.
2. Radical students and faculty focus attention upon some few of the extra-educational activities as evidences of the university's positive support for a controversial and evil government policy. Transmission of class standing to draft boards supports the Vietnam war. Acceptance of contract research on counterinsurgency supports the reactionary imperialism of the United States abroad. The university's real estate dealings discriminate against the poor and the Black in the surrounding community.
3. The university defends its activities on the grounds that it takes no position with regard to social or political issues. It leaves its faculty free to teach what it likes, and to do research as it chooses. It opens its doors to speakers of all persuasions and recruiters for virtually any enterprise which is not illegal. Individuals within the university may engage in whatever political activities they like, but for the university as an institution to take an official political stand would be in violation of

its fundamental principles of value neutrality and academic freedom.

4. The radicals reply that the university *is* endorsing positions and policies by its actions, but that it is endorsing the *wrong* positions and the *wrong* policies. What is needed is an about-face, so that the university will throw its considerable prestige and power into the fight against a reactionary establishment.

This debate, in all the many forms it takes from university to university, revolves about one of the oldest tenets of the liberal tradition—the myth of the value-neutral institution. Just as the state, in classical liberal economic theory, is expected to stand clear of the competitive battles waged between firm and firm, or capital and labor, merely maintaining the freedom and order of the market place of commodities, so the university is expected to stand clear of the intellectual battles waged between doctrine and doctrine, dogma and dogma, in the market place of ideas. Its sole function is to regulate the contest, ensuring a place in the debate to every position and every party. The university administration is charged with the responsibility of protecting those within the academy from the repeated assaults by outside critics, while at the same time guaranteeing that absolute freedom of debate reigns within. From this freedom in the market place of ideas, it is confidently believed, the greatest possible advance in truth and wisdom will flow.*

As a prescription for institutional behavior, the doctrine of value neutrality suffers from the worst disability which can afflict a norm: what it prescribes is not wrong; it is impossible. A large university in contemporary America simply cannot adopt a value-neutral stance, either externally or internally, no matter how hard it tries. This observation is scarcely original with me; indeed, I should have thought it was a commonplace of social analysis. Nevertheless, it is so often and so willfully forgotten that a few lines might profitably be spent demonstrating its truth.

Let us begin with the university's relation to society. A large

* For a critical analysis of John Stuart Mill's famous defense of this thesis, see my *The Poverty of Liberalism*, Chapter One.

university, in respect of its employees, faculty, students, land holding, endowment, and other material and human resources, is in many ways comparable to a large corporation. Columbia University, for example, is one of the largest property owners in the city of New York; the University of California must surely be one of the major employers in the state; and cities like Ann Arbor, Cambridge, and Princeton have somewhat the air of company towns. Now, one of the first truths enunciated in introductory ethics courses is that the failure to do something is as much an act as the doing of it. It is perfectly reasonable to hold a man responsible for *not* paying his taxes, for *not* exercising due care and caution in driving, for *not* helping a fellow man in need. In public life, when a man who has power refrains from using it, we all agree that he has *acted politically*. Omissions are frequently even more significant politically than commissions in American politics, for those in positions of decision usually rule by default rather than by consent.* Hence, acquiescence in governmental acts, under the guise of impartiality, actually strengthens the established forces and makes successful opposition all the harder.

For example, let us suppose that a university cooperates with the Selective Service System, motivated in part by a simple desire to be helpful to legitimate government agencies and interested students, and in part by the conviction that deliberate refusal to cooperate would constitute an institutional opposition to the draft which would violate the principle of political neutrality. Obviously, the university strengthens the draft system, positively by its cooperation and negatively by its failure to take the deliberate step of opposition which was open to it. To be sure, public refusal would have a greater political effect against, than quiet cooperation would have for, the government. Hence there must be better reasons for opposition than there are for cooperation. But the reasons need not be overwhelming or apocalyptic, and, in any event, the action, positive or negative, is a *political* act based on

---

* I am referring here, of course, to the well-known theory of "veto groups." For a general defense of this anti-power-elite view of American politics, see *The Poverty of Liberalism*, Chapter Three.

political considerations. No major institution can remain politically innocent in an open society.

When pressed with such obvious arguments, the administrators frequently retreat to the claim that they merely follow the law. Dow Chemical is permitted to recruit because it and its activities are legal. No moral or political judgment is superimposed on the accepted law of the land.

Now, in actual fact, this defense is false, for the CIA recruits freely on campuses even though it admits to repeatedly breaking domestic laws and violating international treaties. But even when true, the defense fails, for we live in a society which pursues policies by enacting laws. Hence, mere obedience to law is at the same time support for established policy. Suppose, to take a case which is presumably no longer possible, that a school in a state which legally forbids marriages between whites and blacks refuses to hire a white scholar on the grounds that he is married to a Black woman. It thereby lends its great institutional weight to the enforcement of an evil social policy, even though it does so merely by obeying the law. There is no difference between this hypothetical case and the case of defense research or cooperation with the draft, except of course that all good white liberal professors and administrators are opposed to the wicked segregation in the South, while many of the same people feel quite comfortable with America's foreign policy or with their own university's behavior in the surrounding neighborhood.

When we turn to the internal organization of the university, we find the same unavoidable evaluative bias. I have already rehearsed the radical complaint that American capitalism prepares young men for the rigors of the corporate world by the lockstep character of education. Whatever one thinks of this view, it is obvious that an institution imposes some set of values on its students merely by requiring that they maintain a passing grade average, attend classes regularly, take examinations on time, and leave after completing an appropriate assortment of courses. To be sure, the vehicle for the imposition of values is the *form* rather than the *content* of the educational process, but the effect is imposition nonetheless.*

An analogous bias is built into the free market place of ideas, which usually pretends to be neutral among competing dogmas and doctrines. By permitting all voices to be heard, the university systematically undermines all those doctrines which claim exclusive possession of the truth and seek therefore to silence opposed voices. By permitting a Catholic to preach his faith only so long as he allows others to preach theirs, one quite effectively repudiates precisely the central thesis of the Catholic Church. This fact is perfectly well understood in countries like Spain, where opposition to the censorship of the Church is a *political* act. It is also understood in Czechoslovakia, or Russia, or China. For some strange reason, American intellectuals cannot perceive that their own commitment to free debate is also a substantive political act, no more neutral than the prohibition of dissent in religiously or politically authoritarian countries.

Finally, every university expresses a number of positive value commitments through the character of its faculty, of its library, even through the buildings it chooses to build. Astronomy departments ignore astrology, psychiatry departments ignore dianetics, philosophy departments ignore dialectical materialism. Universities build laboratories for experimental research, thereby committing themselves to the importance of the scientific enterprise; libraries devote scarce resources to the accumulation of rare and ancient manuscripts; whole faculties are organized to teach and study social welfare, veterinary science, law, or business. Each of these institutional decisions embodies an evaluation which can easily become the focus of a political dispute.

The conclusion is obvious. No institution can remain politically neutral either in its interaction with society or in the conduct and organization of its internal affairs. To pretend otherwise is merely

* Let me say that I *approve* by and large of the values thus imposed. I am personally very strict with regard to lateness of papers and the like. But I recognize that I must *justify* such requirements with an argument and not claim to be neutral on the issues involved.

to throw up a smokescreen; it is a way of rationalizing the value commitments already made, by attempting to remove them from the area of legitimate debate. Students for a Democratic Society speak of the need to *politicize* the campus. Moderate professors and students oppose this *politicization*, which they protest would alter the character of the university for the worse. But the truth is that every campus is now politicized, necessarily and unavoidably. The radicals do not wish to inflict politics on a realm which once was happily apolitical. They only wish to force an awareness of the already political character of the university, as a first step toward changing the policies which the university embodies or pursues.

On the basis of this analysis, it might appear that the university should drop the mask of impartiality, openly acknowledge the political biases implied by its policies and educational practices, and confront the problem of deciding how its political orientation should be determined. That would, indeed, be the honest and consistent course to follow. To be sure, any system of majority rule or collegial decision would still leave members of a dissident minority unhappy at being associated with an institution whose avowed policies differed from their own; but that must inevitably be true in any case, and at least the policy would be openly and fairly arrived at.

However, the honest and consistent course is not always the best; and I am persuaded that in the United States, at the present time, such a course would have reactionary rather than progressive consequences. There are two reasons why radicals would be ill-advised to expose the incoherence and hypocrisy of the doctrine of institutional neutrality. In the first place, faculties and student bodies tend, by and large, to be conservative in their leanings; and once the university is forced to bring its policies out into the open, the majority is liable to move the direction of those policies even farther to the right. Students are always surprised to discover the melancholy facts of faculty-student conservatism. Since the liberals and radicals on the campus make most of the noise and grab most of the headlines, it is easy to be fooled into thinking that the campus is a hotbed of radical conviction barely contained by a manipulative and repressive administration. Inevitably, the day of disillusion arrives when a faculty vote or student referendum reveals the radicals to be in a distinct minority.

I confess that during the tumultuous events of Spring 1968 at Columbia, I permitted myself to hope that the forces of progress had acquired sufficient support to carry a meeting of the faculty. Each time we were convened, however, the pro-administration bloc defeated the challenges of the rebels by a two-thirds majority. Even in the faculty of Columbia College, a number of whose members had been beaten by the police during the two raids, there was not even a large minority for motions of censure or expressions of opposition to President Kirk's actions. In the end, we had our greatest effect through informal channels of discussion and pressure, where intensity of concern could in part compensate for lack of numbers.

It would be tactically unwise, therefore, to push to an open vote such matters as university acceptance of defense research or the policy of open recruiting. But this is hardly the greatest danger which the politicization of the university invites. Far worse is the ever-present threat of pressure, censorship, and witch-hunting by conservative forces in society at large. The universities at present are sanctuaries for social critics who would find it very hard to gain a living elsewhere in society. Who but a university these days would hire Herbert Marcuse, Eugene Genovese, or Barrington Moore, Jr.? Where else are anarchists, socialists, and followers of other unpopular persuasions accorded titles, honors, and the absolute security of academic tenure? Let the university once declare that it is a political actor, and its faculty will be investigated, its charter revoked, and its tax-exempt status forthwith removed. How majestic and unassailable is the university president who protects his dissident faculty with an appeal to the sanctity of academic freedom!

It is a bitter pill for the radicals to swallow, but the fact is that they benefit more than any other segment of the university community from the fiction of institutional neutrality. For the present, therefore, I would strongly urge both students and professors to hide behind the slogans "lehrfreiheit" and "lernfreiheit," and give up the attempt to politicize the campus. If this advice is too cautious to satisfy their revolutionary longings they may look on the universities as those protected base camps which, Mao Tse-tung tells us, are the foundation of a successful protracted guerrilla campaign.

B. THE MYTH OF RELEVANCE

The plea of value neutrality is the characteristic defense of the academic establishment when its external or social activities are attacked. The call for *relevance* is the characteristic demand of the radicals when they turn their attention to university education itself. Not only is the *form* of education manipulative and constricting, with its constant tests, lockstep course requirements, artificially induced competitiveness, and systematic denial of the spontaneous or idiosyncratic. The *content* as well merely closes the minds it should help to open. The subject matter is abstract and impersonal; it is determined by mandarin traditions designed more to strengthen the supremacy of the senior professors than to enlighten the mind or gladden the heart. Wherever life threatens to intrude on scholarship, it is stifled by "the discipline." Behaviorism in psychology, quantitative methods in sociology, new criticism in literature, linguistic analysis in philosophy—everywhere technique is raised from the status of means to the pedestal of end-in-itself. Whenever possible, the real world is ignored. Where it cannot entirely be suppressed, it is embalmed by the academic undertakers and laid out for observation, looking quite lifelike but safely dead.

Obviously many criticisms interact in this indictment of university education, but they can conveniently be subsumed under the general heading of *irrelevance*. Increasing numbers of the best college students find that their studies have no discernible relation either to their own feelings and concerns or to the great social problems which dominate our public discourse. What do the history of the Hundred Years' War and the reinforcement schedules of pigeons say to a young man who seeks simultaneously to settle the dilemma of his own identity and to advance the cause of social justice? How can a young woman generate enthusiasm for demand curves when she is confused and angered by our society's contradictory attitudes toward intellectual development in women? The demand for a relevant education is frequently directed at two related features of much undergraduate instruction: the isolation of the several disciplines from one another, and the concentration upon technique and detail which appears in the more advanced courses of study. Students counter by calling for problem-oriented, interdisciplinary programs in which a minimum of attention is paid to the history and methodology of each specialty. The ideal course, from this point of view, would be a study of the urban ghetto, with field trips and guest appearances by non-academic experts, drawing simultaneously on materials from history, sociology, literature, psychology, politics, anthropology, and philosophy. Ironically, the radical criticism of the content of higher education echoes the convictions of the greatest native American liberal, John Dewey.

I feel myself deeply divided on this issue of relevance. My own education was a perfect example of all that the radicals reject. Save for several required survey courses in social sciences and humanities, my entire undergraduate career was devoted to mathematics, physics, logic, and the most professionally oriented study of philosophy. I did not so much as read an economics, sociology, or psychology book until after I had received my doctorate. My acquaintance with the social sciences came from the experiences of teaching them at Harvard and the University of Chicago. Such knowledge as I have of literature I owe to my marriage to a literary scholar, not to any course or distribution requirement.

My teaching, by contrast, has been almost entirely in the border areas between philosophy and the social sciences. I have taught the history of Western civilization, introduced undergraduates to social studies, and participated in the planning and teaching of interdisciplinary programs at these universities. One would think that I could be counted on to support the demand for problem-centered, interdisciplinary, relevant education. And yet, I have grave doubts. Perhaps I can best express them by continuing to speak in this very personal way about my own intellectual development and observations.

The portions of my education which proved most useful to me in my attempts at social criticism have been precisely those which originally seemed least relevant to politics or society. The mathematical logic to which I devoted so much time served as the basis for my study of game theory, which in turn enabled me to criticize the technical arguments as well as the moral presuppositions of the defense intellectuals. Without that background, I, like so many other peaceniks, would have been reduced to complaining that Herman Kahn and Thomas Schelling are nasty men, which as it happens is both false and irrelevant to the merits of their positions. My extremely abstract and specialized work on the philosophy of Kant has been the source of my analysis of the foundations of the authority of the state. It is only a short and easy step to a quite "relevant" critique of the notion of civil disobedience and the obligation to serve in the armed forces. The essays I published recently on the nature of liberty, loyalty, political power, tolerance, and community trace their origins to technical studies in theory of knowledge and metaphysics.

When I turn to the social critics whose work I admire, I find the same grounding in a technical mastery of some academic discipline: Kenneth Boulding, Milton Friedman, and Robert Heilbroner are economists; Herbert Marcuse is a philosopher; Barrington Moore, Jr., is a historian; Paul Goodman started his career as a literary critic; and David Riesman came to sociology from the law. No original thinker, it would seem, *starts* with an interdisciplinary study of immediate social problems. Each man or woman approaches society from some discipline, through whose concepts and methods the problems of society can be seen in a new way. Social criticism, in a sense, is an achievement, not an enterprise; it is the outcome of an intellectual activity which is guided by some combination of disciplinary methodologies.

Needless to say, a social critic need not have a Ph.D. in each of the disciplines on which he draws, or in any of them, for that matter. But when we are planning an undergraduate education, it does seem to me that a course in theoretical economics will do more to prepare a student for a socially relevant life than a course on poverty; and a mastery of logic will pay off more handsomely than a seminar on the philosophy of war.

It is not hard to see the rationale behind this apparently reactionary stand. Society and its problems are in perpetual flux. A student who reads books devoted to the solution of present problems will learn nothing which can help him to identify and solve future problems. Insofar as he restricts his attention to the *application* of disciplinary techniques to social problems, he will never learn how to develop *new* techniques of analysis and criticism. His thought will remain fixated at the superficial level of immediate response to daily events. This is what is meant by the pejorative adjective "journalistic." By contrast, the original and important intellectual work always proceeds at a considerable distance from immediate problems, and for that reason frequently seems "irrelevant" or "abstract."

Still the question remains: How can you get the bright, concerned student to sit still for the technical study which alone will prepare him for genuinely relevant work later on? To a generation of young men and women who have sacrificed grade school for the promise of high school, and high school for the promise of college, this can only sound like one more deferral of a gratification which seems ever to recede. Must they postpone their critical analysis of society until all passion has died in them and they have reconciled themselves to the tedium of the academy? I don't know the answer, save to say that honest, brilliant, dedicated teachers will always evoke interest and application from their students no matter how abstruse the subject matter of their courses. But be that as it may, the next generation of social critics will *not* come from interdisciplinary, problem-oriented educational programs, no matter how lively the social conscience which informs them.

C. THE MYTH OF EFFICIENCY

Universities are institutions, and as Erving Goffman has shown in his striking comparison of convents, boarding schools, mental hospitals, prisons, and other "total institutions," the *institutional* character of an institution plays a larger role in determining its internal organization than the particular purpose for which it exists.* Universities may be educational institutions, but like corporations, government bureaus, or armies, they rally to the cry of all bureaucratic bodies: *Efficiency*.

Taken abstractly, the principle of efficiency is innocuous, unexceptionable: Whatever you want to do, use the method that costs you the least, *however you wish to calculate cost*. Do you want to travel from New York to San Francisco? Take the plane, if time is worth a great deal to you; take a train, if you value safety; drive, if you place a premium on scenery, or freedom, or privacy. Whatever it is that has value or "utility" for you, choose a means of action which brings you the most of it or costs you the least of it. And if you value both speed and privacy, or safety and scenery, a formula can be worked out to combine the two in the biggest available "payoff" of "utilities."

Leaving aside some important objections which can be raised against even this broad form of the principle,** we can take it as generally accepted that "efficiency" is desirable in the conduct of any institution. Unfortunately, when we try to translate the demand for efficiency into actual operational procedures for a university, all sorts of absurd consequences result.

Calculations of efficiency require some objective, quantified measure of costs, payoffs, and probabilities, in terms of which the "most efficient" policy can be identified and put into operation. In business, for example, the capitalist calculates the production level and price at which he maximizes profits, and then—if he is rational—comes as close to them as possible. So long as he can predict his sales at differing price levels and calculate his cost per

* See "On the Characteristics of Total Institutions," in Erving Goffmann, *Asylums* (New York: Anchor Doubleday, 1961).

** There is an appallingly extensive literature on this subject, much of it technically formidable. The ramifications reach into theoretical economics, nuclear deterrence theory, psychology, and many other fields. For an example of a negative view of the principle of efficiency see M. Allain, "Le comportement de l'homme rational devant le risque: Critique des postulates et axioms de l'école Americaine," *Econometrica*, vol. 21, pp. 503–546.

unit at different production levels, he can derive a profit curve which tells him what to do.

Now strictly speaking, the same calculation is possible no matter *what* we value. When Jesus says, "What profiteth a man if he gain the world and thereby lose his own soul?" he is, in effect, expressing a certain cost-effectiveness calculation based on the infinitely high value of Salvation. More mundanely, a man who declines a higher profit because it will cost him free time is simply indicating that at a certain point, an additional increment of free time is worth more to him than an additional increment of money. But when administrators attempt to apply the principle of efficiency to the operation of their institutions, they have a natural tendency to measure efficiency in terms of whatever they can quantify, rather than measuring it in terms of what is genuinely related to the real goals or values of the institution. They act like the drunk in the old joke who searched for his watch under the street lamp because that was where the light was best, not where he lost it.

For example, consider the vexing problem of admissions procedures (a subject which is gone into at great length in the next chapter). Elite colleges and universities receive many more applications for admissions than there are places to be filled. Hence an elaborate admissions procedure is developed, relying upon transcripts, letters of recommendation, test scores, samples of written work, and personal interviews. Conscientious administrators anxiously seek for a policy which will be both *just* and—in terms of the goals of the institution—efficient. So far, so good. No one can quarrel with justice and efficiency. But how can the *efficiency* of an admissions policy be measured? Presumably an efficient policy is one which selects those applicants who will prove to benefit most from the educational opportunities offered in the university.*

Now the real problem appears. On any conception of education which goes beyond mere certification or the accumulation of facts

---

* I omit any discussions of the problem created by a *conflict* of goals, such as the conflict between the goal of education and the goals of fund raising and athletic eminence. The confusions over efficiency which I am analyzing exist even in schools which guide themselves by the goal of education alone.

and skills, it is extremely difficult to judge whether an educational experience has been successful or not. The effects are subjective, varied, frequently latent for years or even decades. I can see now how profoundly I was affected by the mathematical logic I studied as an undergraduate, but no test could be devised which would have shown then what its effect would be on me now. Sometimes the nature of an educational experience is *negative*. A student discovers that he *dislikes* a subject, or is *not* enlightened by a particular approach. It is extremely important for him to learn that fact, but what measure will distinguish between his fruitful negative encounter and another student's mere failure to make genuine contact with the professor or subject matter at all?

Baffled by such subjective ambiguities, when he is aware of them at all, the dean of admissions falls back on the measurable: What percentage of the freshman class graduates successfully four years later? Now there's a fact a man can sink his teeth into. Clearly when five thousand apply and one thousand are admitted, something is wrong if five hundred of the thousand drop out. An admissions policy which lets in only two hundred dropouts would be "more efficient," and a perfect score of one thousand graduating seniors indicates a maximally efficient policy. Or so it would seem. Alas, a perfect score may actually reveal a dismally unsuccessful admissions policy. The thousand may merely be candidates so attuned to the educational experiences of the college that they encounter no challenges, take no risks, and fail to change in any significant way during their four undergraduate years. In that case, their education has been a failure, even though not a man has dropped out. The student who never receives his degree may actually benefit more than the student who stays on through graduation.

Note: I am not saying that it is sometimes better for a student to drop out. That is of course true, but it is a relatively modest claim. I am saying that in terms of the goals of the university itself—namely, education—the dropout may actually have learned more *by dropping out* than the "successful" student learned by staying. In such a case, applying the criterion of efficiency, we should put the dropout in the profit column and the degree holder in the loss column. An admissions policy which picked the dropout would be *more efficient* than one which didn't. Yet, is there a dean of admissions in America who could contemplate a dropout rate of thirty or forty or fifty percent with equanimity and believe that he had an efficient procedure?

The same irrelevant calculations crop up in other branches of the university's activities. At Columbia (and for all I know, at other universities as well), a department's allotment of graduate fellowships is heavily influenced by the number of doctorates it has "produced" in the preceding several years. As I write this, I learn that my department will be permitted to offer a large number of fellowships to this year's applicants because we have given more Ph.D.'s than usual lately. It is natural for the head of the Fellowships Office to guide his distributions by such criteria. After all, he is not competent to judge the *quality* of the work done in philosophy, or physics, or history. What else can he go by than numbers?

Suppose my colleagues and I discover that fully half of next year's students are intellectually and temperamentally unsuited for careers in philosophy. If we conscientiously discourage them from continuing, thereby performing one of the most valuable and difficult of all educational tasks, we shall constrict our "production" and lose fellowships in years to come. On the other hand, if we see the unfitted candidates through the doctorate, thereby acting in an *educationally* inefficient manner, we will be rewarded with fellowships, additional positions in our staff, and even salary raises.

The craziness of this procedure is still marginally apparent at the level of the individual department or teacher. I know that some of my students have failed to benefit educationally from my courses, even though I give them passing grades and send them along to the next stage in their careers. My department certainly knows that some of the doctoral candidates inflating our production figures would be better off in other lines of work. But by the time the figures have all been collected and passed up to the highest administrative level, all life and reality have been squeezed out of them. From the president's office, where broad university policy is made, little is visible save statistics—percentages of drop-outs, numbers of doctorates, a growth rate in masters' degrees, credit-hours per professor in the sciences or the humanities. Naturally enough, top administration judges itself—and is judged by others—on the basis of its ability to run a tight ship, an efficient operation. Education is the goal, to be sure; but it is degrees, scholastic aptitude scores, and Nobel Prize winners that can be numbered.

To all this, the administrator may reply, What else would you have us do? We are not philistines. We do not confuse bricks and books with the growth and liberation of the mind. But *some* decisions must be made about hiring, building, admitting; some plan must be adopted for allocating the scarce resources of the university. Since you admit that true educational success is difficult to judge and impossible to measure, your romantic cry from the heart leaves the real decision makers like us right where we were. Until you offer a better rule, I will continue to admit students who are likely to graduate and assign fellowships to departments which produce Ph.D.'s.

A fair challenge. There is no virtue in the mock purity of ir-responsible criticism. If the utopian like me has no alternative *even in theory*, then he ought not to indulge in the frivolity of attacks on the managers of established institutions. I shall propose a general principle for the making of administrative decision in educational institutions, but I do not expect administrators to accept it. Indeed, I doubt that they will even view it as a *principle* at all, for it contradicts the very essence of the administrative mode of thought and action. My principle is this: Make adminis-trative decisions in educational institutions *subjectively*, not *objec-tively*. Consult those persons who seem to *you* most truly imbued with what *you* conceive to be the essence of education, and then follow your instincts. If it is a matter of admissions, admit a class of students who *smell* right to you, and don't worry about justice, efficiency, or the dropout rate. If you act on this principle, your institution will be biased, idiosyncratic, risky, quirky, unbalanced, not at all every man's cup of tea—but it just possibly may also be a place where genuine education flourishes. I have always suspected that something like this happened at the University of Chicago under Hutchins. Judging from the descriptions I have heard, I would not have been happy there. I am suspicious of Great Books; I have no use for Thomism, secular or otherwise; I detest the practice of examining by "objective" tests; and I am put off by intense, snobbish intellectuality. But everybody I have ever met who taught or studied at Chicago during those great days agrees that it was the most exciting educational experience of his life. What is more, those people all strike me as vitally alive intellectually. If Hutchins had striven for balance, justice, efficiency, and value-free objectivity, Chicago would probably have been one more dull, homogenized American university.

Ironically, paradoxically, there are some human activities in which subjectivity is more efficient than objectivity, in which calculation kills and instinct inspires. Art and love are notoriously of such a nature. I believe that education is also.

CHAPTER THREE

The Admissions Rat Race*

In 1950, 2,214,000 students were enrolled in American colleges and universities. By 1960 the total had grown to 3,570,000 and projections for 1970 range as high as seven million. This increase is not merely a consequence of the growth of the American population. Of 1,000 boys and girls in the fifth grade in 1942, only 205 entered college in 1950. But of 1,000 fifth graders in 1954, 336 entered college in 1962. By the time the present grade-school children have reached college age, the proportion may exceed one-half.

The consequent rise in college applications has of course been

* This chapter first appeared in *Dissent*, Winter 1964, under the title "The College as Rat-Race: Admission and Anxieties." It has since appeared in revised form in *Atlantic Monthly* Magazine in November 1965 and has been anthologized several times.

distributed unevenly among America's colleges. Although there are still many accredited institutions which begin the year with room in their freshman classes, the elite schools—the Ivy League, the seven sisters, the best state universities—are faced with many times the number of students they can accommodate. The result has been a fundamental reorientation in the attitude of colleges toward the selection of students. Instead of setting admissions *requirements*, they have to develop an admissions *policy* by which to choose from among the excess of well-qualified applicants.

The applicants fall readily into three groups: the clear admits, the clear rejects, and (characteristically) a large middle group of possible admits. In this third segment are to be found the students with strengths and weaknesses which must be weighed against one another and translated into a one-dimensional scale of preference. Should the college admit a boy with strong but not spectacular grades and little evidence of independence, or the boy (from a different kind of school and background) whose relatively weaker but not disastrous grades are balanced by signs of creativity and ambition? Should the admissions committee deliberately strive for a heterogeneous freshman class, or judge each case purely on its merits without reference to the character of the other applicants already admitted?

The situation is aggravated by a number of interactions between the colleges and the high schools. Students, aware of the increasing difficulty of obtaining admission to their chosen schools, begin to make multiple applications in order to protect themselves. The result is an inflation of applications to the best colleges, forcing them to estimate the percentage of admittees who will actually show up in September.

Simultaneously, the "college advisers" in high schools and preparatory schools, alerted to the problems in the colleges, begin to discourage students from applying to schools to which they have little chance of being admitted. This entirely laudatory move merely worsens the problems for the colleges, for it reduces the number of "clear rejects" in the file of applications, leaving a still more unwieldy group of "possible admits" from which to select a freshman class. The colleges also experience considerable anguish at the thought of gifted students being discouraged by uninformed college advisers.

Meanwhile, the colleges have been making their task still more difficult by their attempts to adopt objective, nonparochial criteria of admission. It is true that athletic ability, the right prep school tie, or an alumnus father will improve a student's chance to get into many schools. But as applications mount and colleges strive to improve their student bodies, these factors play a decreasing role in admission decisions. By and large, the men who run the admissions offices of the top schools are dedicated to the principles of fairness and equality of opportunity which serve Americans generally as ideal standards. Their quite admirable dedication merely intensifies the problem of selecting an entering class from the mass of applicants.

At this point, a different and originally separate factor in American education comes into play: the increasing use of aptitude and achievement testing. The Educational Testing Service first administered the Scholastic Aptitude Test, or SAT, in 1926, almost forty years ago. In that year, only 8,040 students took the examination. In 1961–62, this figure had increased one hundredfold to 819,339. Virtually every applicant to a good college or university now takes the SAT, and large numbers take achievement tests in particular subjects as well.

The SAT is an objective examination of the multiple-choice type. The faults of such tests are too well known to require rehashing. What is less well appreciated by laymen (although this is clearly understood by admissions officers) is that strictly speaking, the Educational Testing Service does not even *claim* to be measuring intellectual capacities such as intelligence, creativity, receptivity to new ideas, or the ability to see conceptual relationships. It only claims to measure the probability that a student will do well in college. It is, one might say, an extrinsic, or black box, prediction. Students who do well on the test tend to do well in college. This may be because the test measures capacities which are later drawn upon by college work. Or it may be because the test measures exam-taking ability, which also serves the student in college. In any event, it is a statistical fact that the probability of a good college record is higher for the student with a high SAT score.

The test is far from accurate, however, even in terms of its own criteria. According to the 1961–62 annual reports of ETS, the divergence of any given score from the "true" score (i.e., an average over a long period of time of a student's scores on similar tests) is on the order of 30 points two thirds of the time. That is to say, "if a student's 'true' score is 500, the chances are two out of three that the score he will actually make on the SAT will be between 470 and 530." Out of every six students, one will probably score more than 30 points above his "true" score, and another probably more than 30 points below.

If multiple-choice tests are suspect in themselves, and if their accuracy as predictions of college success is far from adequate, why are they used so extensively by admissions officers? There appear to be three reasons:

First, and by far the most important, is the admissions officer's need for some way of comparing the cases in his burgeoning file of "possible admits." Fairness and the bureaucratic strictures of committee work require him to produce reasons for favoring one candidate over another. When the dossiers are mixed bags of strengths and weaknesses, it is in practice impossible to defend one's ordering of five hundred or a thousand cases without reference to some sort of objective criteria. The SAT serves as just such a measure.

Closely related to this is the desire of admissions officers to reduce the percentage of admits who flunk out later on. The SAT claims to predict college success: deans are haunted by the possibility that a good and potentially successful student will be turned down in favor of one who eventually fails to complete the college course. Since deans (and professors) by and large conceive of success in education as a matter of grades, credits, and degrees, such a case appears to them to be an educational failure. A low percentage of dropouts is considered a sign of a good admissions program.

Finally, as the average SAT scores of incoming freshmen classes rise at the elite schools, ambitious colleges begin to treat the scores as a sign and measure of their own place in the educational system. A rise of 50 points in the freshman average is used by recruiters as an additional inducement for prospective students and their parents. What began as a means of handling a swollen tide of applications becomes in the end a measure of educational status.

Here, as with the pressure of admissions itself, there is feedback to the secondary school level. Parents quickly become informed (and misinformed) about the importance of "college boards." Pressure is put on high schools to coach the college-bound seniors in the mysteries of multiple-choice tests. Despite ETS's insistence that careful research reveals the futility of such preparations, classes sprout in SAT-taking. Soon, high school *juniors* are submitting to "Preliminary SATs" whose purely tentative results are then used to guide the students in their college choices. As figures pile up, tables are constructed showing the statistical relationship between junior and senior SATs. Indeed, ETS tells us that it is "possible to make similar estimates of senior-year SAT scores from the scores on the School and College Ability Test (SCAT) taken even earlier. There are tables which provide these estimates based on SCAT scores as far back as the eighth grade." (ETS report, 1961–62, p. 35.)

The ever-earlier testing is merely the most striking element in the frenzied business of college preparations. Students are exhorted by parents and teachers to raise their grades. The colleges, which have never based their decisions solely on academic achievement, begin to emphasize "extracurricular activities," and as the news filters back to the high schools, teenagers are hastily enrolled in dance classes, music lessons, outing clubs, and intramural sports. The colleges counter with a search for signs of individuality and originality; desperately teenagers are pushed into beekeeping and piccolo playing. And so it goes, on and on—colleges searching for ways to sort the applicants and predict their college careers, students desperately twisting themselves into what they hope will be appealing shapes, anxious to be singled out from the crowd of fellow students.

What has been the effect of the endless testing and evaluating on our high school boys and girls? First of all, the ever-present imperative to "do well" in an objective and measurable way is intensified, to the detriment of real education, or even of non-"educational" growth experiences. Americans have come to treat education as a process of homogeneous, crisis-free absorption of information and development of skills. The irregular, the irrational, the unconforming, the random, is seen as a *failure* of education. The only difference between the traditional and progressive attitudes is that the first blames these aberrations on the student while the second blames them on the school. That they are undesirable is never questioned.

But as so many perceptive observers of adolescents have pointed out, growth from childhood to maturity is *necessarily* ungainly. It is the trying on of ideals and life styles, the committing of new found emotional energies. As Erik Erikson has shown us through his study of Luther, the "identity crisis" of late adolescence or early adulthood is positively *creative*, and certainly not an embarrassing misfortune to be excused and quickly suppressed.

Unfortunately, the college race has just this repressive effect on many of the most intelligent and sensitive—hence vulnerable—youngsters. Experiment and commitment require a willingness to accept the possibility of failure. They demand an incautious, even imprudent singleness of purpose. The wise counseling and anxious hectoring of the college-mongers is death to experiment.

In his junior year in high school, John, an "A" student, becomes fascinated by boats. He spends hours at the docks, quizzing sailors about their tasks, cadging rides on tugboats, dreaming of distant places. For a year he is completely wrapped up in the sea. Then, abruptly, the passion leaves him and he puts behind him as childish the dream of becoming a sailor. He has tentatively tried on a role, given himself up to it, and found that it does not answer to his needs. The year has been immensely valuable to him as a stage in his growing up. But it has been a disastrous year at school. Absorbed in sea charts and sailing manuals, he has had scant time for history, French, math, and physics. In his record there is no indication of the milestone which this year has marked in his life; only the low grades, dropping his cumulative average below the "top college" level. Discouraged by the unaccountable slump of a promising student, John's college adviser directs him to a solid local state college. The competition is so stiff for admission to the elite schools that there seems no point in his trying to overcome the handicap of that junior year.

John has been hurt by the system, for the education available to him at the top schools really is superior to that offered by the local college. But at least he has had his junior year, and he will be a better man for it. Far worse off are the other young men and women who have been cajoled or harassed away from creative adolescent commitments by their parents and teachers. In the name of a "good education" in the future, these well-meaning adults stifle the good education of the present. The energies which should be used by boys and girls for growth are instead diverted to useless and deadening "college preparation."

Aware of the tragedies of secondary education, many colleges have begun to make room in their admissions policies for a controlled measure of irrationality. Each year, a school will accept a certain number of applicants who defy all their objective criteria, but simply "smell right." Admirable as such risk-taking is, it has no effect on the high school student, for he cannot be sure that he will be one of the mavericks who is saved by an intuitive dean. If the internal dynamic of his growth carries him outside the limits of secondary-school acceptability, he must be prepared to forfeit the race to college.

The successful college applicant has thus frequently mortgaged himself to the future, sacrificing a genuine education in high school in order to obtain a superior education in college. What does he find when he finally enrolls at the school of his choice? No simple description can be given, any more than for the high school, but again trends are visible which are deeply disturbing. Until a very few years ago, the entering freshman at any of a number of top colleges would have been confronted with a mixed program of broad survey courses designed to make him "liberally" or "generally" educated, more specialized courses from among which he could select a sample, and in his last year or two, a departmental "major" requiring him to concentrate on a single discipline. In addition, he would have the opportunity to do independent research, usually as a means to a degree with honors. The premises of this sort of undergraduate program were basically two: first, that the typical freshman had not yet had a chance to roam at will in the realm of ideas, acquainting himself with the excitements and potentialities of the intellectual life (I remember my astonishment when, as a freshman, I discovered that there was a field of knowledge—sociology—which I had not even known to *exist!* It was like discovering a new color, or better a whole new sense); and second, that several years should be given over to relatively uncontrolled experimentation before a young man or woman was required to make a decision about a career.

In the past decade, however, both of these premises have been yielding to pressures from below and from above. The General Education movement is under severe attack at Columbia, Chicago, and Harvard, the three schools which have done most to foster it. The causes are complex, involving problems of personnel and administration as well as of educational principle. One reason is that good high schools have instituted "advanced placement" college-level courses using many of the same books which appear on the General Education reading lists. Consequently, more and more students have had the material by the time they reach college. Now just what it means to have "had" Dostoevsky or Freud or Marx is, of course, problematical. It may mean that the student has read works by the author, brooded over the ideas, and grown through his struggle to understand them. It may also mean that he has been intellectually immunized by being inoculated with small, weakened dosages of the author. At any rate, the well-prepared student can pick the right answer out of five choices an adequate number of times, and so he is assumed to be generally educated.

In response to the improved preparation of the freshman (which manifests itself in better language, math, and English composition training as well as in advanced placement courses), the colleges decide to "enrich" the undergraduate curriculum. The job is turned over to the departments, or—at universities—to the graduate faculties, whose general view of undergraduate education is that it is a watered-down version of graduate education. Everywhere the same solution is hit upon: give the bright, able, well-prepared undergraduates a first-rate training in some graduate department. Administratively, this amounts to listing graduate courses in the undergraduate catalog and requiring the concentrator to take baby generals and write baby dissertations. At a school like Harvard, for example, a senior honors thesis in history may be a 150-page research monograph, and the honors generals in English demand a professional mastery of large segments of the literature of the last millennium.

At the same time, pressures of military service, postgraduate professional training, and the cancerous growth of specialized knowledge, place a premium on choosing a career early. The sciences have long insisted that they cannot give adequate graduate training to the college graduate who has not already tucked some of the requisite material into his mind, and medical schools of course set "pre-med" requirements. But now the same song is sung by economists (who fancy themselves really mathematicians), psychologists, philosophers, and historians. As the undergraduate population swells, the admissions squeeze reappears at the best medical, law, and graduate schools. Once more, the education of the present— for which the student gave up so much in high school—is sacrificed to the demands of the future. Eager to relax and reap the fruits of his race to college, the student must climb onto the treadmill to graduate school.

But here the race for education ends. Upon entering graduate school, the student—now an adult—is told that his education lies *behind* him. From this point on, his intellectual and spiritual maturity is taken for granted. Graduate schools do not educate the whole man; they train the specialist. So it seems that somewhere, somehow, the successful student has lost an education. Always it was before him, over the next exam, beyond the next degree. Now suddenly it is behind him, and that unique moment of potentiality in the growth of the soul is gone.

What has gone wrong? The answer is simple: Each present was sacrificed to the future, until the presents were all past, and the future an empty present. It is a familiar enough story in our society. We call it prudence, or deferral of gratification, depending on our tastes in moral discourse.

What can be done? Alas, the answer is not so simple. It won't help to administer the system with more intelligence, awareness, compassion, and imagination. These qualities are already in surprising abundance among the educators of our country. The solution, if there is one, must cut to the root of the problem. It must reverse the order of priority, and at every stage subordinate the education of the future to that of the present. A good high school experience must count for more than admission to a great college. An exciting college education must in turn take precedence over preprofessional preparation for postgraduate training. How can this be done?

First of all, there is no point in demanding that college admission procedures be made *fairer*. The harm they inflict on high school students does not flow from their imperfections. It flows from their very existence. So long as the education in our colleges varies widely in quality, and admission to college is based on an evaluation of precollege performance, parents and teachers will push students into a competition for admission. Nor should we issue pious warnings to high school students about the dangers of listening to their elders. They do not yet have the inner resources to withstand the threats and seductions of the adult world. Indeed, their spiritual growth demands identification with precisely those individuals who are encouraging them to compete. The adolescent student is faced with an impossible dilemma. If he accepts the values of his elders, he loses his chance for real growth and instead climbs on the treadmill. But if he shies away from the grade race, where else is he to find the adult figures through identification with whom he can realize himself? As Paul Goodman has pointed out, the only alternative is to retreat into a sterile, adolescent world of beats or gangs.

The solution to the problem, if it exists, must be institutional. The temptations of the admissions race must be destroyed. So far as I can see, there are two ways in which this might be done, neither of which will meet with instant acclaim. Either the value of admission to one college rather than another must be eliminated; or admission to college must be made an irrational process on which the student can have no influence. The first could be achieved by a nationwide forced homogenization of institutions of higher learning, the second by assigning high school graduates to colleges at random. Both alternatives have analogues within the educational world. The academic high schools of a large city system like New York are kept approximately equal by budget allotments and the policy of teacher assignment. Most students then go to the school in their district. And many colleges assign their students to dormitories at random, for the very sound reason that competition for rooms would lead to discrimination, jealousy, cliques, and all the unpleasantness associated with fraternities or private clubs. My personal preference is for a process of random admission. It is by far the easier of the two to administer, and could be instituted immediately.

In the concluding chapter of this book, I will indicate some practical steps for implementing this proposal.

PART THREE

How Should a University Be Governed?

CHAPTER ONE

Why Should a University Be Governed at All?

At the heart of every revolution is a challenge to the political authority of the rulers. The revolutionaries may focus their criticism on the particular policies and practices of the rulers—there may be a list of "grievances" or "demands." But the aim is not merely redress of grievances, or satisfaction of demands—the ultimate goal is a shift of the locus of legitimate authority in the community.

This proposition is as true of student rebellions as it is of the great revolutionary movements of the past two hundred years. Protests against ROTC, Dow Chemical recruiting, or secret research tend to turn into attacks on the legitimacy of the university administration. To be sure, the administration's readiness to cooperate with an immoral foreign policy may be put forward as evidence of the moral failure of the president and trustees, but that moral failure in turn is taken by the rebels as a ground for the "de-authorization" of the university rulers.*

It is for these reasons that university discipline so often arouses passions all out of proportion to the apparent importance of the

---

* The term "de-authorization" comes from Lewis Feuer's *The Conflict of Generations* (New York: Basic Books, 1968), a psychosocial historical study of student rebellions here and abroad. Feuer's general thesis is that student rebellions are basically generational conflicts in which the sons attack the authority of the fathers. Despite the weakness of Feuer's treatment of the American experience, and his rather unfortunate political biases, the book is an important contribution to our understanding of university rebellions.

issue. At Columbia, for example, the demand for "amnesty" for the demonstrators very quickly became the real obstacle to a compromise settlement of the original dispute. It was easier to persuade the trustees to back down on the famous plan for a gymnasium in Morningside Park than it was to get them to agree to a dropping of criminal charges against those arrested in the police actions. More generally, the issue of university governance—who shall make such decisions as are made at all in the university community—lies at the heart of most of the campus disputes in recent years.*

We could dispute endlessly over the relative merits of a strong presidency versus a strong board of trustees, or over unicameral versus bicameral academic senates. Much also could be said about the details of disciplinary tribunals and the role of due process in the internal affairs of a university. But after roughly a year of such debates at Columbia, I am persuaded that they generate no light, and after a while fail even to radiate much heat. The fundamental question can be stated much more simply: How should a university be governed? But before that question can be answered, there is a prior question which must be asked: *Why should a university be governed at all?*

An odd question, perhaps. Surely every institution must be governed! If there are roles, rewards, established practices, decisions to be taken and implemented, then some rules must operate for determining who fills the roles, who receives the rewards (and suffers the penalties), who makes and enforces the decisions. That is just what is meant by a "government." So corporations, unions,

---

* There is one significant exception to this generalization. The demand for more Black teachers and a larger enrollment of Black students is not in the first instance an attack on the *authority* of the university. Rather, it is a demand for a reallocation of scarce resources—money, jobs, places in schools. As such, the demand falls well within the limits of ordinary interest-group American politics, and it will almost certainly be met, as all such demands are met, by a partial adjustment which gives the Black students some of what they want. The "rational" rather than "symbolic" character of the Black demands was evident at Columbia, where the behavior of the Black students in Hamilton Hall contrasted sharply with that of the white SDS students.

hospitals, churches, armies, even private clubs and fraternal organizations, all have some form of government.

Nevertheless, let us indulge the philosopher's penchant for asking questions that no one else would think to answer. *Why* should a university be governed at all? In developing an answer to this peculiar question, I think we can set the stage for a full-dress review of the major alternative answers to our basic question, *how* a university should be governed.

One point of clarification before we begin. We are concerned with the problem of *authority* in a university, not with the quite different question of *power*. *Authority* is the *right* to command, and correlatively it is the *right* to be obeyed. Many men make claims to authority. Presidents, dictators, generals, saints, fathers, princes, doctors, all claim to have the right to be obeyed. Sometimes the claim is based on genealogical succession, sometimes on professional expertise, sometimes on divine sanction or even the force of personality. These days it is most common to rest one's claim on the supposed consent of those commanded. But whatever the basis, the content of the claim is the same: I have a right to issue orders, and you have an obligation to obey them. Obviously, not all claims to authority are valid; but a surprisingly large proportion of authority claims win acceptance from those over whom they are made. People really do follow kings into battle and saints to the cross. Somewhat more routinely, modern men habitually follow the directions of anyone who dresses in an official-looking uniform or carries official-looking papers. So our question concerns what we might call *de jure*, not *de facto*, authority. We want to know how a university *should* be governed, not how as a matter of fact universities *are* governed.*

In the political sense of the term, authority is a relationship between persons. To be sure, we sometimes say that a man *is an authority* on something, meaning that he knows a great deal about

---

* The subject of political authority is too important to be dealt with in this summary fashion. For an extended discussion of the foundations of *de jure* authority and a defense of the principle of philosophical anarchism, see my "Political Philosophy," in *The Harper Guide to Philosophy*, edited by Arthur Danto (to be published by Harper and Row).

it. But no one would seriously maintain that expert knowledge of a field gives a man the right to *command* others. At best, we might say that it was extremely *imprudent* to ignore the counsel of an "authority." To say that a man *has authority*, on the other hand, is precisely to say that he has the right to make decisions or issue commands and that others have an obligation to obey him.

A university is (or, more precisely, ought to be) a center of research and education. Research is essentially an activity involving only one person, though it is frequently conducted in groups. We must look to education, therefore, if we are to discover the natural locus of authority in the university. What are the basic educational relationships in a university?

There are, I suggest, *three* different sorts of educational relationships which may exist among the members of the university community. The first is the relationship between an accomplished scholar and a student who wishes to become a scholar. I have already characterized this as analogous to the relation of apprentice to master craftsman. The scholar has mastered a form of intellectual activity which the student seeks to learn. Since no codified set of rules of procedure can successfully capture the craftsmanship of the master, the student must actually try his hand at the enterprise—be it historical research, chemical experiment, or philosophical argument—under the guidance of his professor. Gradually, the student progresses from the stage of relatively easy tasks set and corrected by the teacher, through attempts at simple works conceived by the student but executed under the professor's eye, to the final performance—the dissertation—whose successful completion proves the student's competence to be counted among the masters of the profession. (Hence the term "master work," or work which earns one the title of master). Needless to say, this idealized description bears only a distant and accidental similarity to what actually goes on in graduate schools; but it is, I think, a correct account of the ideal educational relationship of professor to graduate student.

The second educational relationship, characteristic more of undergraduate than of graduate life, is the relation of a mature and developed intellectual to a young man or woman still in the process of intellectual development. There are emotional as well as intellectual elements here—an identity crisis may be involved, certainly a process of identification and internalization is essential. The teacher communicates skills, to be sure, but more importantly he communicates an attitude toward skill, as well as attitudes toward clarity, honesty, responsiveness to evidence, a concern for relevance. In short, the teacher, when he is successful, teaches values. Except that he may teach them best by never mentioning them! A university is then not only a place where potential scholars can find actual scholars; it is also a place where young people can find mature men and women who live by the Socratic dictum that the unexamined life is not worth living. It is a natural setting for the intellectual growing-up which ought to accompany physical and emotional growing-up.

Finally, in a university we find educationally important relationships among students at every level of development, and analogous relationships among scholars and teachers. Very little need be said about these relationships, save that they are the real life of the university community. It is a commonplace that the most valuable educational asset of an elite Ivy League school is neither the distinguished faculty nor the lavish physical plant but simply the quality of the student body.

If authority has a place in the educational relationships of the university, then it must be in one or more of these three relationships that it will be exercised. So our next question is simply this: In which of these educational relationships is there an appropriate exercise of authority?

To put my case as simply and forcefully as possible, the answer is: *None. Claims to authority, the exercise of authority, and submission to authority have no place whatsoever in any of the characteristic educational relationships of a university.* Let us consider the relationships in turn:

Clearly the relationship of a scholar to apprentice can involve no element of command or obedience. If the apprenticeship is to be at all successful, the student must freely choose to follow the scholar's directions, reserving always to himself the right to sever the relationship should it seem to him unhelpful. The same freedom must belong to the scholar. He rejects candidates whose promise he judges inadequate, and at any time he must have the right to decide that a student has failed to develop the qualities of intellect required for continued fruitful study.

To be sure, the student may seek out a professor who is, in his view, "an authority." But any such seeking-out implies that the student is judging the professor, not *vice versa*. Can anyone seriously imagine a professor *commanding* his student to continue a line of study which the student has firmly decided to give up? Does it make sense to speak of a student as "obligated" to obey his professor, in the way that we speak of citizens as obligated to obey the law? A teacher may be a "tyrant," "a dictator," an "autocrat" —no one who saw Toscanini rehearse an orchestra would imagine that he ran it on the principle of participatory democracy! But submission to such "authority" is always free, voluntary, and revocable at will, which is to say that it is not *submission to authority* at all.

What is true of the scholar's relation to his graduate students applies as well to the undergraduate teacher's relation to *his* students. Indeed, the strong affective component in the relationship makes success depend even more heavily on a mutually voluntary basis. The student must be free to choose his teacher—and that means free to reject him as well. The teacher too must be free to reject a student, though he may rarely if ever exercise that option. This freedom is the foundation of the relationship—it is the bond which holds them together and makes each willing to work so hard with, and for, the other. If I know that my students have chosen to study Kant's ethical theory with me, that they have come to me out of a desire to learn and a conviction that I can teach them, then I will spend any number of hours necessary to master the texts, think through my interpretation, and prepare my lectures. I will be endlessly patient with the student who does not follow my argument, and honestly responsive to questions which I have difficulty answering. But let me discover that the students are merely taking my course to fulfill a requirement or get a grade, and the heart goes out of my teaching. It becomes a deadly chore, about as satisfying as making love for money!

There are a great many pedagogues who will dispute these remarks, I imagine. Freedom is very nice, they will say, but a good deal can be taught and learned even under the severest of constraints. After all, though youngsters are required by law to attend primary and secondary school, one must admit that they frequently learn something. Higher education is not compulsory, true; but in the hierarchical Roman Catholic world, even the most distinguished professors of theology submit themselves to the authority of the Church without thereby destroying the intellectual merit of their scholarship. So make a plea for freedom if you will, but do not claim that education is impossible without it!

Since I *do* claim that education without freedom is impossible, I had better say a few words about why I maintain so extreme a thesis. My argument turns, of course, on what I mean by "education." Obviously a man can "learn" languages, mathematics, science, history, literature, even philosophy, no matter how servile his mind. But what exactly does it mean to say that he has "learned"? Does it mean merely that he can repeat some proposition, answer questions about it, get it right on an examination? If so, then knowledge has nothing to do with freedom. Or does it mean that he can give *reasons* for what he believes, that he can himself see the merits of those reasons, and that he stands ready to withhold or change his beliefs whenever he judges it right to do so? If *that* is what "learning" means, then authority and education are polar opposites. Authority says, Do this, believe this, because I say so! Education says, Here are reasons for doing, for believing—reflect on them and see whether you yourself judge them to be good reasons.

Socrates was quite correct when he argued, two and a half millennia ago, that a teacher never truly teaches his student. The teacher can assist the student to learn by suggesting arguments, pointing to facts, raising questions which the student has not noticed himself. But if the education is to be genuinely successful, the student must freely adopt the conclusion as a result of his own understanding of this truth. Ironically, this ancient truth is most obvious not in the branches of learning known as the humanities, but rather in pure mathematics. In a mathematics class, the professor goes over each proof in the hope that the students will see why the conclusion follows from the premises. A poor student may, out of desperation, memorize whole proofs for the final examination, even though he does not grasp their logical connections at all; but no one would say he had thereby *learned* any mathematics. Indeed, the manifest inappropriateness of authority-claims in mathematics helps to explain the fact that older mathematicians so readily defer even to the youngest student when he comes up with a new and demonstrably valid theory. The more patriarchal humane disciplines would do well to imitate mathematics in this regard, for it is the mark of genuine intellectual freedom.*

What is true of the relationship between teacher and student, it goes without saying, is true as well of the relation between student and student or teacher and teacher. Education takes place in such relationships only when they are founded on a mutual freedom of association. I conclude, therefore, that so far as the educational function of a university is concerned, no issue of *government* in the customary political sense can even arise. Educationally speaking, the answer to the question, How should a university be governed? is simply: It shouldn't be. Or, more precisely, It can't be, for any attempt to impose a structure of authority on truly educational human relationships must either fail or else succeed merely in making education impossible.

* It follows from the above that Catholic theologians *cannot* truly be said to *know* what they believe so long as they submit themselves to the authority of the Church. They may be learned, distinguished, full of years, and heavy with honors, but unless they make themselves the final judges of the propositions to which they assent, they remain more ignorant than the beginning goemetry student who will not say Q.E.D. until he sees why the theorem follows from the axioms. The great *philosophes* of the Enlightenment understood well enough the conflict between ecclesiastical authority and intellectual freedom, but it has become fashionable recently in agnostic intellectual circles to adopt an attitude of sympathetic approval toward so-called "liberal" movements in the Catholic Church. Men who would rather burn their manuscripts than submit them for some official Imprimatur speak glowingly of such autocrats as the late Pope John, who was, after all, quite as ready as the present pontiff to demand obedience to the official dogmas of the Church. I am afraid that I can see no greater merit in submission to Rome than to Moscow or Peking. One ancestor of the Quotations of Chairman Mao, after all, is the catechism of the Catholic Church.

But universities *are* governed. They do have presidents, boards of trustees, senates, regulations, disciplinary tribunals. So it will not do to suppose that we have settled the matter. If a university, in its educational aspect, neither needs nor indeed can permit a structure of authority, then we must ask what *are* the functions or activities in virtue of which authority enters the academic setting? So far as I can see, there are four areas in which universities claim and exercise some sort of authority. These are: *first,* in the quasi-parental dictation of students' living arrangements; *second,* in the external relations of the university, including the economic administration of an endowment; *third,* in the admission and certification of candidates for degrees; and *fourth,* in the employment of faculty and other personnel and the collection and distribution of student fees and subsidies. None of these has directly to do with education at all, but since they are the areas in which the dispute over university authority arises, we must examine them if we are to come to any conclusions about the principles of university governance.

As we approach the final quarter of the twentieth century, I trust that we need spend little time debating that burning issue of American Victorianism, "Women In The Dorms." Today's students have earned the right to be treated as adults rather than children, and though somewhere in the backwaters of higher education a panty raid or fraternity pledging prank may still provide the principal excitement on warm Spring evenings, more serious problems have taken center stage.* Let us agree that students ought to man-

---

* Strictly speaking, students are somewhere in between childhood and adulthood, as I have already pointed out. One way of accommodating our institutions to that fact would be to adopt Margaret Mead's proposal that there be two sorts of marriage rather than only one. The first would be entered into or dissolved at will but would not carry with it the right to have and raise children. The second, with rather stricter criteria both of contracting and of dissolving, would be reserved for those men and women (of whatever age) who were ready to make the life commitments necessary for the creation of a stable home in which to bring up children. The point is that students are quite mature enough to make their own personal and sexual decisions, but their status as students conflicts with the starting and raising of a family. Since in the last chapter I propose that students be permitted to omit college

age their own living arrangements, including dormitories, cafe-
terias, general rules of decorum, and so forth. This is not to say
that a college dormitory must be like an apartment house. The students and faculty of a college may collectively desire the benefits
that come from some more closely integrated form of living. They
may wish to unite into a genuine community, with communal
meeting room and dining halls, and some form of dormitory self-
government. In that case, the only general rule is that the members of the community must all participate in its management.
Obviously there are certain objective constraints here as in the society in general. If one generation of students votes to live in dormitories, the next generation cannot casually decide to scrap the
dorm and live in the surrounding town or city. The endowment of
the school will be frozen in those dorms, and not even the wealthi-
est school can change its bricks and mortar from year to year. But
let us leave such details to one side. In all matters pertaining to
student (and faculty) living arrangements, the university community as a whole has a right to exercise collective decisory authority,
but obviously neither the faculty nor the administration has any
right to dictate such decisions to the students.

Genuine problems swarm into view as soon as we turn to the
university's relationship to the outside world. The major question
for private universities, of course, is the management of the endowment. Time was when this matter could be left in the presumably
capable hands of a small group of wealthy alumni who, as trustees,
would administer the portfolio and real estate holdings of the university. But no longer! With endowments ranging in size up to the
one billion of Harvard, and with urban schools like Columbia
dominating the composition and growth of their surrounding communities through real estate acquisitions, the decisions concerning
the endowment now head the list of issues in contention.

Well, who *should* hold final authority in this matter? The question is a peculiar one no matter what your social philosophy. It

---

before going on to professional training, if they so desire, the restriction of
child-rearing marriages would not force a young man or woman to wait three
or four years. It would simply force a choice between the adult commitments
of parenthood and the exploratory openness of the search for identity.

seems quixotic to suggest that the management of some hundreds of millions of dollars be vested in a student body the majority of whose members cannot legally control their own property. Should a student passing through a university for three or four years really participate in decisions on which the entire future of the university may depend? And yet it is equally absurd to assign these crucial powers to a group of academically undistinguished alumni who exhibit no particular understanding of the life of the mind and whose principal utility is as potential donors to a fund drive.

Who owns a private university, after all? The trustees? The alumni? The faculty and students? The society at large? The peculiarity of the question suggests the anomalous status of our greatest educational institutions. The subject of endowment management is too complex to be explored here. At the very least, however, it should be clear that the critical economic decisions of the private university can no longer be left in the hands of a small group of businessmen, however wise or prudent, who answer to no one for their actions and bear no integral relation to the educational activities of the university.

A host of other prickly questions come under the general heading of "external relations." I have already said something about them in my discussion of the myth of value neutrality and in my attack on the ideal of the multiversity. My primary concern here is not to issue a number of *obiter dicta* on ROTC, contract research, IDA, and campus recruiting, but rather to focus on the problems these issues raise for the proper governance of the university. As we have seen, the peripheral accretion of programs, institutes, and extra-educational activities has turned universities into conglomerate holding companies with lines of authority so tangled and diffused that executive decisions can in practice be made only at the very top. At Columbia, for example, no one disputes the faculty's authority over purely instructional matters, but these days it seems as though those matters occupy a mere corner of our lives. Law professors do not claim authority over the requirements for the Bachelor of Arts degree, any more than medical students demand a voice in the course content of the School of Architecture. The confusion and the conflict begin when someone in the Administration makes a decision about cigarette filters or CIA recruitment. Suddenly the entire university community finds itself implicated in an action which it neither initiated nor approved. Presidents and trustees never hesitate to speak and act in the name of their universities, but it is hard to see what right they have to do so.

All of these problems take on a different complexion when the university is supported directly by public rather than private funds. I confess to a deep-seated prejudice in favor of private institutions, on the grounds that they are freer of political manipulation and invasion, but that may simply be because in the United States wealthy businessmen from old Protestant families have proved to be stauncher defenders of liberty than state senators and representatives. Nevertheless, we are clearly in the age of the public university, and something must be said about the principles which should govern such an institution.

The natural view is of course that since the people pay the bills, they should through their representatives govern the campus. Unfortunately, the present state of public attitudes makes that principle a guarantee of disaster. When the "level of political consciousness" has been raised, then the campuses can be safely ruled by the people's representatives. For the time, however, I think state universities would be well advised to cultivate whatever measure of autonomy their academic status and institutional insularity can win for them. The rule must be, Act as though you were a private university, and try to get away with it!

Certification raises problems of authority which lie at the heart of the university's educational life.* Dormitories, endowments, and recruiting on campus are, after all, extraneous to the university *qua* university. Many schools have no dormitories or endowments, and the university could continue its essential activities even if no recruiter ever set foot within its walls. But certification is another matter entirely. One might almost *define* a university as

---

* Under certification I include examinations, grading, the determination of course content, and in general everything which can be considered a part of determining "the requirements for the degree of ———," as the college catalogs put it.

an institution empowered to confer higher academic degrees, and the conferral of degrees means the exercise of the authority to certify. So in countless commencement exercises, the president intones, "By the authority vested in me . . ." as he formally confers the degrees on the several candidates.

Now certification, as we have already seen, performs a social and economic, not an educational, function. The medical student does not experience a surge of surgical skill as the ceremonial hood is placed about his neck. What he receives is the medical faculty's official and public announcement that he has fulfilled the requirements laid down by law and the profession, and is now competent (after certain further ordeals) to practice medicine in the United States.

If the sole purpose of certification were to attest to an acquired competence, there would be no problem at all in determining who should have the authority to do the certifying. Obviously the authority would reside in general in those already certified, and in particular in those who have directly instructed and tested the candidate. But the major function of certification, either directly or indirectly, is to regulate the allocation of young men and women to extremely desirable jobs carrying high salaries and status. Hence complex considerations of justice and social welfare arise which may take precedence over purely professional determinations of competence. Suppose, for example, that the medical profession sets its standards so high that only a handful of superbly qualified doctors come out of the medical schools each year. Public welfare may require the state to force the medical faculties to lower their standards, on the utilitarian grounds that a larger number of less able doctors is preferable to an insufficiently numerous elite of specialists. So too, social justice may demand that a preferential system of admissions for minority candidates be adopted in teachers' colleges, simply in order to increase the number of Black and Puerto Rican teachers in urban schools.

Students also may have a right to share in the authority over certification, not because they already possess the requisite competence, but merely because their economic future depends upon the certifying process. This is a tricky issue, and I shall try to sort it out more adequately in the next chapter, but it is important always to remember that the question of authority in the classroom *never* arises in an educational context. It arises *only* in the context of certification.

We come finally to what might be called the "economic" function of a university—its role as an employer of teachers and a purveyor of educational services to students. Many of the touchiest questions of authority arise in this area, including that tenderest of all matters, the promotion to tenure of junior faculty. It is a historical accident (though *not* historically accidental) that the university is an employer of teachers and a collector of student fees. The Socratic model of the economically independent teacher with his aristocratic pupils remains, in my view, the proper ideal of education. The flaw is not in the model but in a world which permits only the wealthy few to adopt the model as their guide.

Ideally, a teacher should have some means of livelihood which is completely independent of his activity as a teacher. He ought to choose to teach because he wants to transmit what he has learned to others, and his success or failure as a teacher (not to speak of his popularity, which is another matter entirely) should have no bearing on his income. Correlatively, students should seek out teachers because they wish to learn, not because they need point-credit for salary raises or degrees for certification. They should be accepted as students on the basis of their ability, interest, and commitment, not because of their ability to pay tuition and to forego other income which might be earned in the same time. (Inasmuch as these two propositions are merely obverse and reverse of the same coin, it is striking that the first sounds wildly utopian while the second is almost universally accepted as a commonplace in advanced industrial societies.)

Historically, a variety of social arrangements have been employed for supporting university teachers. Aside from the Socratic method, which has thus far enjoyed very few imitators, we can note the custom of church support, which has its roots in the Middle Ages and continues to flourish today in Catholic colleges and universities. German universities adopted the institution of *privatdozenten,* licensed teachers whose fees came directly from students rather than from the university. In a communist society of the sort envisioned by the young Marx, we would return to the Socratic ideal. Wealth would be distributed according to one's need rather than in proportion to the market demand for one's services, and teachers would teach, as writers would write and painters paint, from love for the activity itself.

But America is neither a theocracy nor a communist utopia, so university teachers, like other workingmen, earn their living by doing their job, which is teaching.

Critics of university education very rarely reflect on how much of the day-to-day business of the academy is determined by this commonplace fact. For example: if men are going to earn their living as university teachers, then simple economic justice demands that they be able to acquire some job and wage security. Life tenure is obviously not essential on purely economic grounds, though I see no reason why professors should throw away that enormous fringe benefit at just the stage in history when it is first being won by longshoremen. But *some* contractual assurance of employment is clearly a legitimate demand for professors to make of their employers.

Now, as soon as you grant this stability of wages and employment, you place constraints on the educational offerings of the university. The ideal may be absolute freedom for teacher and student, but economic reality dictates constraints on both sides. Professors can be required (or, if they are tenured, cajoled) to teach courses which are "needed," despite their total lack of interest in the subject matter. And students can be presented with a catalog of course offerings which bear a tangential relation at best to their current interests. Size of classes, frequency of meetings, vacation periods, and so on, are all determined by economic rather than educational factors. In its hiring and promotion policies, departments pay considerable attention to "balance" or "distribution," primarily because of their certificatory responsibilities. One of the most familiar problems facing a faculty is the choice between two junior professors, both admirable scholars and teachers, who are so unfortunate as to specialize in the same field.

Because of the virtual irrevocability of tenure, the promotion or appointment of a professor to a tenured rank is the most important single decision ever made in a university. Curriculum innovation, building programs, disciplinary procedures, even the selection of a president, can in time be reversed, but when an assistant professor rises to the rank of associate professor with tenure, very little short of his retirement save certified death can remove him from the faculty. Under present career conditions, this means that the tenure decision carries a thirty- or thirty-five-year commitment. A man who attained tenured rank near the end of the Great Depression would only now be approaching the age of retirement, and in the customary gerontocratic order of the university, he would be at the height of his influence. Much of the innate conservatism of universities is traceable to this fact of academic life.

Summarizing what we have said, questions of authority and government do not arise naturally in the context of purely *educational* relationships. They pertain to the university *as an institution* insofar as it performs four noneducational functions, viz: the oversight of students' private lives *in loco parentis*; the commitment of the university to relationships with the external world, including the management of an endowment; the certification of candidates for degrees; and the employment of faculty and purveyance of educational services to students.

CHAPTER TWO

How a University Should Not Be Governed

How should a university be governed? Our answer will obviously depend on what goals we think a university ought to pursue. In Part One of this book, we analyzed four competing models of the university, each built on a different conception of the purposes or ends of the ideal university. Now we can associate a different principle of university governance with each of the four models.

If we interpret the sanctuary for scholarship as including within it the sort of undergraduate education just sketched in the preceding chapter of this section, then the appropriate principle of governance is clearly *anarchism,* or no rule at all. Authority simply does not pertain to educational relationships or activities as such.

The model of the university as a training camp for the professions seems quite naturally to imply the principle of an aristocracy of competence. "Aristocracy" *means* "rule by the best," in this case the best professionals, not the morally best as in Plato's Republic.

Clark Kerr has himself told us the political principle of the multiversity: it is democratic pluralism, the received doctrine of contemporary establishment political science.

Finally, the anti-ideal of the university as a staging area of revolution embodies the political doctrine made popular by the theorists of the New Left: participatory democracy.

Leaving anarchism to one side as a nonprinciple, let us examine each of these proposed rules of governance in turn.

1. ARISTOCRACY OF COMPETENCE AS THE PRINCIPLE OF AUTHORITY IN THE UNIVERSITY

If the university is to serve as a training camp for the professions, then questions of legitimate authority would appear to resolve themselves quite readily. The primary function of such a university is to train candidates for the professions and then admit them to active practice by certifying them as competent to perform the professional duties required of them. Clearly, the standards of professional competence can only be set and applied by members of the profession who have already demonstrated their own competence. Who but doctors can determine what a medical student ought to know before he may be permitted to undertake his own practice? Would anyone seriously propose that lawyers define the standards for a degree in engineering, or that physicists examine the candidates for a doctorate in English literature?

Common sense requires, in addition, that relative superiority of competence be acknowledged within the ranks of the profession. The medical examiners should be chosen from among the most accomplished doctors, not from the margin of the profession where the barely competent linger. Exactly the same principle covers the conduct of the academic profession in the performance of its certificatory duties. Logicians certify students of logic; romance philologists certify candidates in French language and literature; and whenever possible, certification is overseen by outstanding logicians and romance philologists, not merely by hack practitioners.

The arguments which exclude one profession from infringing upon the authority of another apply with equal force to students vis-a-vis their mentors. If a Nobel Prize–winning physicist with a classical education and a rich appreciation of European culture has no business intruding on the certifying procedures of the Department of History, it goes without saying that a twenty-two-year-old graduate student of indifferent intellectual attainments has no such right either. The demand of students for a role in the certification decisions of their professional school or department is entirely contrary to the principles of professional competence. There may, here and there, be a student already possessed of fully enough knowledge and skill to qualify him for certification, who merely awaits the formal recognition by his profession. But the typical student, by hypothesis, lacks the competence required by the accomplished experts in his vocation. If he did not lack it, he would not be a student!*

It follows that when degree requirements are set, faculty are hired or promoted, examinations are graded, and students passed or failed, final authority should rest in the hands of the masters of each field whose proven competence equips them to pass judgment on the qualifications of prospective practitioners. What is

---

* In "soft" fields, like my own field of philosophy, it is common for students to claim a competence equal to that of their professors, or even to deny that any objective criterion of competence can be defined at all. In this way, such students merely exhibit their contempt for their own field, since none of them would dream of suggesting that mathematics or medicine was equally "subjective." My own observation suggests that the experts in a field have very little difficulty in distinguishing genuine competence from gross incompetence, no matter whether the field is romantic poetry or plasma physics. Marginal distinctions are of course disputable in all fields.

more, the preponderance of authority belongs by right to the ablest members of the profession (regardless of age).

In short, the slogan of the professional university is, All power to the senior faculty! The students, who have been chosen by competitive criteria of ability and preparation, are expected to submit to the authority of those men and women whose demonstrated competence defines the standards of the profession to which the students aspire to be admitted. The administration, insofar as one is required at all, ought to be a servant of the faculty, for *as* administration it lacks the knowledge to define or enforce professional standards in a university.* If it seems unjust that some should rule and others obey, we need only remark that each member of the institution passes through all the stages of authority during his career. No man or woman is born to the senior faculty, and no competent student is condemned for life to the student class.

The principle of academic aristocracy will of course be challenged by anyone who denies that professional training is the sole, or even the primary, purpose of the university. But even if we grant that premise, the argument for aristocracy can be subjected to an attack which, in my opinion, demonstrates the need for major concessions to student demands for a share of decision-making authority. The basis of the attack is the fact that universities are not isolated institutions operating in a social vacuum, but are parts of a totality of social institutions whose impact on students is systematic rather than atomic.

The point can best be made by means of an example from a different sector of university life—the discriminatory fraternity or social club. On many campuses, in the Ivy League as well as in the

---

* This dependent status is sometimes symbolized by permitting deans to sit in a faculty only in their role as professors, not *ex officio.* I confess a sentimental attachment to such manifestations of faculty supremacy. Much of what is wrong with American higher education could be corrected if only faculties felt that jealous pride in their collective authority which ennobles parliaments and craft unions. After all, the President of the United States must formally request permission to address the Congress; I see no reason why the President of Columbia should not be required by the faculty to exhibit an analogous deference.

Big Ten, students run highly selective social organizations which offer their members eating, sleeping, and recreational facilities, friendship, and even a file of term papers for last-minute assignments. The clubs are self-governing, and they restrict membership on every conceivable basis: sex, wealth, race, religion, social position, even academic distinction.

Taken in isolation, there is no reason at all why such a club should not operate on any discriminatory principle it chooses. White Protestants have a perfect right to segregate themselves behind closed doors, and so do wealthy Catholics, Orthodox Jews, Black Nationalists, athletes, or scholars. But on some campuses, a system of such clubs develops which comes to dominate the social arrangements of the entire student body. In many schools, for example, all social life goes on in fraternities or sororities; and no alternative facilities exist for those who are excluded either by choice or prejudice. In such a situation, the excluded student has a legitimate claim on the *system* of fraternities and sororities as a whole, even though he cannot prove an a priori right of admissions to any one of the organizations *in particular*. So long as fraternities are to be the basis of male social life on campus, he has a right to be admitted to some fraternity or other; and the student body as a whole has a general right to a share in deciding how the fraternity system shall function.

A case in point is the system of Princeton eating clubs which is at last beginning to crumble. For a very long time, the eating clubs were the only decent, attractive, convivial accommodations available to a Princeton undergraduate. The few freshmen whose religion or color made them totally unacceptable to the general run of Princeton gentlemen were forced into makeshift eating arrangements on the periphery of the college's social life. Eventually, protests (and the embarrassing Ivy League custom of admitting socially unacceptable young men merely because they are brilliant) forced the creation of a club specifically designed as a "feeder of last resort," to paraphrase an expression familiar to students of unemployment. Obviously such a situation is thoroughly unjust and ought to be abolished. But the injustice does *not* inhere in the discriminatory practices of any particular club. Equally restrictive clubs exist at Harvard with no injustice whatsoever. The injustice inheres in the *system* of clubs at Princeton; it derives from the fact that at Princeton (but *not* at Harvard), the clubs so dominate the life of the college that a student has no adequate alternative mode of life and recreation available to him.

Consider now the position of a young man or woman confronting contemporary American society. As our economy operates, wealth and security sufficient for an attractive life are in general dependent upon success in some professional or quasi-professional career. The traditional professions—law, medicine, teaching, engineering—of course require certification by an established institution of professional training. In addition, a bachelor's degree has come to be viewed as a prerequisite for admission to junior executive or executive trainee slots in business firms. Generally speaking, higher education is the gateway to comfort, leisure, status, and security in America.

From the point of view of any particular college or professional school, the applicant is a free agent who has sought out the institution and requests admission as a means to the pursuit of his own ends and purposes. No applicant has any *right* to be admitted to a particular school, nor does he have a right vis-a-vis a particular school to participate in the formulation of the curriculum or standards. To put the point crudely, the medical school has not *asked* the applicant to apply, any more than the fraternity has asked the freshman to present himself for admission. If the faculty of the professional school wish to set extremely high standards or emphasize branches of their discipline which the applicant would rather not study, it is not *they* who stand under an obligation to change.

But when we look at the situation from the point of view of the high school senior applying to college and the college senior applying to graduate school, we see an entirely different picture. We see a nationwide *system* of universities and colleges, not a heterogeneity of discrete institutions. It is true that the applicant has no special claim on Harvard or the University of Michigan or NYU, but does he not have some sort of claim on the totality of higher education? After all, he is coerced by his society quite as thoroughly as the Princeton freshman is by the eating-club system. He has no alternate route leading to middle-class America. A young man or woman cannot become a doctor without attending college and then studying at an accredited medical school. The practice of apprenticing aspiring lawyers in law offices has disappeared, and even the business world requires formal credentials from those who seek places in the great corporations.

To be sure, colleges and universities vary. Reed College is not CCNY, and Yale University Law School offers greater scope than Harvard Law for the sociologically or philosophically inclined candidate. But these variations are confined within a very narrow uniformity of educational programs across the country. We tend to forget how artificially constricting it is to make *every* student move through twelve years of primary and secondary schooling, four years of college, and then two (business) or three (law) or four (medicine) years of professional training.

When men's vital interests are coercively affected to a major extent by the operation of a system of social institutions from which they cannot escape, it seems to me reasonable to assert that they acquire a right to participate in those decisions of the system which affect them. This right does not derive from their competence or from their experience, but merely from their entrapment within the system of institutions. The Harvard freshman has no right to a voice in the policies of the Harvard clubs because the "society" of Harvard undergraduate life offers him adequate alternative means for satisfying his physical and social needs. The absence of such alternatives creates such a right for the Princeton freshman.

Analogously, American undergraduates (*and other* young people not enrolled in colleges) have a right to share in the determination of the curriculum and certification procedures of their preprofessional and professional training. Their right is not grounded in any special wisdom they possess. It does not flow from the fact, sometimes cited in this regard, that they are particularly well-placed to judge their teachers; nor have they yet acquired the knowledge needed to make informed judgments about curricula and standards. Their right stems solely from the fact that society offers them no genuine alternative way to prepare themselves for productive and rewarding lives.

Even if this argument for student power is accepted, it is very difficult to see exactly how it can be translated into workable proposals for a distribution of decision-making authority. Higher education in America is a system in the sociologist's or economist's sense of an interacting multiplicity of social units which exhibit law-like uniformities of behavior and norms. But it is *not* a system in the legal or political sense of a centrally controlled institution with explicit legislative and executive procedures. Leaving to one side state or national certifying agencies in the professions (such as state bar associations, the American Medical Association), there is no national body with the authority to regulate the curricula of particular colleges or oversee the hiring and firing policies of individual faculties. There is nothing analogous to the Congress, representation in which would give students as a class some say over the society-wide educational policies to which they are subject. If students are to share in the decisions which determine the content or form of their education, they must do so within the institution where they happen to be enrolled. Indeed, since the heterogeneity of our system of higher education should be increased rather than curtailed, any attempts to centralize decision making in order to provide an appropriate location for student influence would be disastrous. America would find itself moving in the direction of the worst features of French, German, or Russian education.

Under the circumstances, some compromise must be struck between the certificatory authority which belongs to a faculty aristocracy of competence, and the rights which belong to students entrapped in an educational system to which there is no social alternative. Ideally, education should be divorced from professional training, and professional training in turn should be divorced from certification, so that society offers a maximum of freedom, variety, and individual determination consistent with the protection of the public from sheer quackery and fraud. At least some steps in that direction are possible even within the existing framework of the American economy and educational system. In Part Four, I shall sketch those steps and indicate my reasons for advocating them. But so long as universities do serve as training camps for the professions, the inductees must have a say in the conduct of their basic training.

2. DEMOCRATIC PLURALISM AS THE PRINCIPLE OF AUTHORITY IN THE UNIVERSITY

Since Clark Kerr sees the modern multiversity as a reflection in miniature of the heterogeneity of American society, it is not surprising that he takes over the standard theory of American government as his model for its internal governance. The multiversity "is not one community but several," he says [p. 18]. Just as America is a plurality of religious, ethnic, geographic, economic, and cultural communities in dynamic interaction with one another, so the multiversity is a multiplicity of subcommunities—schools, departments, faculties, student bodies, administrators, nonacademic employees, alumni—which impinge on one another, compete for scarce resources, pursue diverse goals, enter into shifting alliances with each other, and all insist that each is the *real* university.

The theory which analyzes and justifies this sort of political community is commonly known as Democratic Pluralism. It is a modern variant of classical democratic theory, adjusted both to fit the facts of advanced industrial society and to meet objections to the earlier model of pure parliamentary majoritarian politics. In an earlier book, I have analyzed democratic pluralism in some detail; my conclusion was that it is imperfect as a description of the actual process of politics in America, inadequate also as an *ideal* toward which we might wish to move, and more often than not an ideological rationalization for certain serious injustices in American society.* This is hardly the place for a full-dress rehearsal of those arguments, so instead I shall confine myself to a number of criticisms of the theory as it applies to the operation of a modern university. Essentially what I want to argue is that a university has

* See *The Poverty of Liberalism*, Chapter Four.

no business governing itself as an interest-group democracy. I won't dispute Dr. Kerr's claim that increasing numbers of schools actually are run that way.

The principal defect of pressure-group politics in the university, as we have already seen, is its failure to distinguish between pressures which one should resist and pressures to which one should yield. When students protest the shape of the curriculum, their voices should be heeded, for the reasons I outlined earlier in this chapter. But when the state legislature demands a more conservative faculty, or the government seeks a home for its military research, the university should dig its heels in and fight for its communal life. Now Kerr, like all democratic pluralists, speaks from time to time as though he accepted this distinction between good and bad pressures, or legitimate and illegitimate interest groups. At one point, describing the tasks of the multiversity president, he even assigns to himself the metaphysical responsibility of "painting reality in place of illusion" [p. 40] to the competing groups in the academy. But in practice, democratic pluralism quickly accords legitimacy to any group which has sufficient money or votes, no matter what its aim. As Kerr says, "[the multiversity] serves society almost slavishly" [p. 19]; he goes on immediately to add, "a society it also criticizes sometimes unmercifully." But as the authors of Roman comedy were fond of showing us, masters can stand a good deal of "unmerciful" criticism so long as they can count on slavish service!*

A second objection to the pluralist mode of governance in the university is its proneness to accept the myth of efficiency as its criterion of educational success and failure. As I argued in Part Two, a falsely quantitative corruption of efficiency beguiles administrators into taking admissions, grades, graduation, and awards statistics as evidence that real education is taking place in their institutions. The University of California is of course notorious in

* I am always amused when one of the flunkies of the Kennedy or Johnson Administration defends his public silence on the invasion of Cuba or the Vietnam war by insisting that he dissented vigorously *within* the councils of government before the decision was taken. What difference does it make to the President how loudly some aide cries, Nay, Nay! in private; all that matters is that he should bray, Yea, Yea! in public.

this regard, with its fetishistic acquisition of Nobel Prize winners, but even Harvard from time to time lets slip the delicious details of the mean scholastic aptitude scores of its incoming freshmen, and City College in New York will happily tell anyone who will listen that more of its alumni hold doctorates than are held by the alumni of any other single college.

Nevertheless, the pluralism of the multiversity encourages this statistical pulse taking for the simple reason that in a heterogeneous community there is no other readily available, agreed-upon measure of success. If the classicists believe that the engineers are jumped-up mechanics, and the educationists think the faculty of arts and sciences is a collection of amateur teachers, and if all of them refuse to admit that library science deserves a bachelor's degree, let alone a doctorate, how on earth can they possibly agree on a multiversity-wide budget? How can they find standards by which to compare the effectiveness of all the programs, schools, and departments which compete for resources in the multiversity? The all-too-natural tendency, alas, is to reduce the disputes not even to the *lowest common denominator*, but merely to the *most available numerical indicator*. Far better indeed to split them apart, send them on their separate ways, and permit each to pursue its own vision of excellence. Some will surely go wrong; others hopefully will flourish. But no central administrator should be charged with the task of deciding which is which.

My last criticism of pluralism in the multiversity will cheerfully be accepted by Dr. Kerr, for he openly asserts it as a *virtue* of his new-style academy. He writes:

> To make the multiversity work really effectively, the moderates need to be in control of each power center and there needs to be an attitude of tolerance between and among the power centers, with few territorial ambitions. When the extremists get in control of the students, the faculty, or the trustees with class warfare concepts, then the "delicate balance of interests" becomes an actual war [p. 39].

This is a description as well as a prescription, for the structure of pluralist politics makes it *probable* that moderates will rule, whether or not it is *desirable*. And that is just the problem. Is it desirable that "moderates" should rule a university?

It depends, I suppose, on what one means by "moderate." If Kerr merely thinks that a university is a better place when wise and reasonable men govern it, then I am hardly the one to disagree. I bow to no man in my respect for reason and wisdom. But if, as his language suggests, Kerr imagines that reason and wisdom lie somewhere in the "middle" of any dispute, then he is sadly mistaken. Where education is concerned, wisdom is far more likely to lie at the extreme ends of the spectrum of opinion than somewhere safely in the middle. When I think of the great teachers I have known and the great scholars whose work I have studied, I find that few of them indeed could be called "moderate," and many would quite naturally fall under the heading "extremist." Does Dr. Kerr imagine that Socrates was a moderate? No one puts moderates to death! (I do not mean to suggest that it is the moderates who *put* people to death. No indeed! Moderates are the people who try to get death sentences commuted to life imprisonment.)

As I pointed out in my critique of democratic pluralism, there is much to be said for the middle road when *interests* are in conflict.* An *interest* is precisely the sort of thing that can reasonably be compromised, for when loaves are being fought over, half a loaf is better than a fight to the death for a whole loaf. But compromise may make no sense at all where *principles* or *ideals* conflict. To take a concrete example, suppose that there is a dispute in a university between those who wish the undergraduate curriculum to be open, unstructured, exploratory, self-developmental, and ungraded, and those who desire a curriculum devoted to preprofessional training.

Pluralists like Kerr would undoubtedly survey the dispute, identify these two views as "extreme" and move tactfully toward a compromise—two years of open-ended exploration and two years of professional concentration, or perhaps a specified fraction of total "credit hours" in one major field and free election of the remaining courses. But such a compromise is almost certain to

* Cf. *The Poverty of Liberalism*, pp. 136–137.

sacrifice *all* the educational benefit of *both* plans. The curriculum will be neither free enough to accomplish the liberation sought by the first faction nor concentrated enough to do the really adequate training sought by the second faction. *It would make much more sense educationally to turn the curriculum over to one faction and permit those students and professors who find it uncongenial to seek a totally different undergraduate milieu elsewhere.*

As a recent presidential candidate quite aptly put it, "Extremism in defense of liberty is a virtue." Of course, he caught hell from the moderates.

3. PARTICIPATORY DEMOCRACY AS THE PRINCIPLE OF AUTHORITY IN THE UNIVERSITY

Like Democratic Pluralism, the principle of Participatory Democracy is a general political principle which is applied by its adherents in many contexts other than the university. In the rapidly changing world of New Left politics, participatory democracy has apparently already peaked in popularity as a rallying cry, but it is so natural an expression of the new wave of radical sentiment that it deserves some analysis and criticism.

The principle in its most general form asserts that when decisions are made which affect people's lives, those people have a right to participate in the decision-making process. As interpreted in particular situations, the principle goes far beyond the purely formal participation of periodic elections, and even beyond the continuous participation offered by interest-group–pressure-group politics. Participatory democracy is a call for a revitalization of the ideal of direct participation. Characteristically it emphasizes decentralization of decision making, community control, local initiative, and a willingness to substitute *ad hoc* procedures of maximum responsiveness for the rigid patterns of traditional politics.

With all of this I am in total agreement. As a firm believer that direct democracy is the only true democracy, and that all other political arrangements are merely more or less benevolent forms of tyranny, I welcome the rebirth of the faith which led Rousseau to say that even the representative government of the English was merely a kind of voluntary slavery. But the principle of participatory democracy itself, when translated into specific proposals for a redistribution of authority, seems to me sometimes incoherent, sometimes incomplete, and sometimes quite unworkable (though as a utopian radical I tend not to weigh this last defect too heavily).

Consider for example how the principle would apply to a graduate department of philosophy such as the one in which I teach. At present, authority for decisions concerning graduate education rests partly with the professors in the department, partly with the Graduate Faculty as a whole, partly with the President and Trustees of Columbia University, and partly with the New York State Legislature (which sets minimum requirements for class hours per accredited course, and so forth). In practice, of course, the department itself makes the day-to-day decisions within guidelines set by the Graduate Faculty; the President, Trustees, and State Legislature are not very much in evidence. Now our graduate students demand a vote (or perhaps a veto) on curriculum, hiring, promotion, and degree requirements. The reason given is the principle of participatory democracy: those who are affected by decisions should share in the making of them.

On the face of it, this is a reasonable demand. Indeed, in my discussion of the principle of an Aristocracy of Competence I argued for something fairly similar. But taken literally, participatory democracy leads to some very odd conclusions. For who is actually affected by a philosophy department's decision to offer a full professorship to an associate professor at another institution? In the first instance, the candidate himself, so he ought to vote on the question. And the other candidates whose names have been passed over in favor of his—so they ought to vote.* Clearly the colleagues at the candidate's present school will be vitally affected, so they ought to vote, as should the graduate students now work-

---

* Anyone who thinks this reasoning fanciful or frivolous simply doesn't know the academic world. When the word gets round that Harvard is looking for a Shakespeare man, or Yale needs someone to cover logic, the potential candidates are quite well aware of the opportunity. Sheer out-and-out *applying* for a top professorship is of course Not Done, but a great deal of delicate jockeying goes on all the time.

ing with him who will lose their dissertation director if he leaves.

Should the graduate students in the department *making* the offer have a vote? Presumably yes, but not those advanced and experienced graduate students who will be getting their degrees before the new man arrives. Surely the college senior who intends to apply for admission to the department should vote, for the future makeup of the department will affect them more than any other single group of persons.

This sounds ridiculous, and so in a sense it is. But it all follows perfectly straightforwardly from the principle of participatory democracy. I have not distorted the principle or carried it to extremes for the purpose of making fun of it; I have simply taken it seriously. In practice, of course, the partisans of Participation do not demand that the decision be shared by all these various groups of interested persons. What actually happens is that the demand is made in the name of any interested group which makes a big enough noise to be noticed. At Columbia, the demand for a vote on appointments came from the graduate students. When it was pointed out that any appointment affected undergraduate education as much as graduate education, they agreed but showed little interest in the fact. If the undergraduates had come forward with their demand for a share of the authority, the graduate students would no doubt have agreed.

In practice, then, the principle of participatory democracy can be rephrased: All those who are affected by a decision *and demand a share in making it* should have that share. But this seems to me totally unacceptable. It substitutes noise and organization for any sort of reasoned principle of apportionment of authority. It does not even embody what might be the most plausible rule of thumb, namely, that one's share in a decision should be proportional to the extent of the effect on one's life.

What is missing from the statement of the principle, though it is quite obviously present in the practical demands of radical students, is some sense of the communal, institutional locus of authority and responsibility. It sounds silly to suggest that professors and students at Michigan vote on a decision at Columbia because, after all, *they aren't members of the Columbia community.* They are affected by what goes on at Columbia, to be sure, but that fact by itself does not give them a right to share in the decision at Columbia.

The true principle of university authority, I shall argue in the next chapter, is that authority resides in the community taken collectively, and that the demand of students for a share of decision-making authority is justified *because they are members of the community*, not because they are affected by the decisions. In a sense, the principle of participatory democracy is an expression of alienation, not a demand for community. It is a protest from those who confront an alien world, full of institutions which are perceived as *other* and which are intrusive, coercive, and harmful in their effects. When men and women find themselves trapped by society, they have a right to demand and to receive some measure of control over its alien decisions. But as a principle of authority for an ideal community, participatory democracy falls far short of the goal at which men should aim.

CHAPTER THREE

How a University Should Be Governed

There are two quite different ways in which the analysis of social institutions can be conducted. The first, which might be dubbed the "Platonic" after Plato's procedure in the *Republic*, begins with the definition and demonstration of ideals, and only then proceeds to grapple with the reality which inadequately embodies them. The Platonic mode of analysis is best suited to reformers and revolutionaries, for the contrast which it presents between what is and what ought to be serves as a powerful motive for social action.

The second mode of analysis, tracing its origin to Aristotle, "looks for the universal in things." It begins with a description of existing institutions, and looks for the ideals which either are actually embedded in them or else are said to be embedded in them.

The "Aristotelian" mode of analysis is very good at discovering ways in which institutions fail to live up to their own ideals, but it takes a "Platonic" approach to show that the ideals themselves need changing.

All of this is merely a somewhat stuffy way of saying that I am going to give two answers to our question, viz, How should a university be governed? First I shall offer my ideal answer—a sketch of the principles of governance of the university that ought to be. Then I shall return to the real world, accept such compromises with the ideal as seem unavoidable on even the most optimistic reading of contemporary affairs, and state how I think a real university in the last third of the twentieth century in America ought to be run. Even this "realistic" proposal will look wildly utopian to many, but there is a limit to how much of the real world a reasonable man can accept and still retain his self-respect. There is, for example, no sensible answer to the question, How should a multiversity be run? except perhaps the flat reply, It shouldn't!

So, first the utopian, then the merely ideal.

1. THE SOCIAL CONTRACT OF THE IDEAL UNIVERSITY

The ideal university, in my view, is a *community of learning*. This phrase, which I take from Paul Goodman, expresses the central fact that a university ought to be a *community of persons* united by collective understandings, by common *and communal* goals, by bonds of reciprocal obligation, and by a flow of sentiment which makes the preservation of the community an object of desire, not merely a matter of prudence or a command of duty.*

* The logical structure of community is complex, involving as it does reciprocal states of awareness in a number of persons. In the concluding chapter of *The Poverty of Liberalism*, I have tried to develop an analysis of the concept of *community*. This discussion of the university as a community is intended as a development and exemplification of that analysis. Notice that genuine community requires each person's awareness of others as conscious agents—hence as persons, not merely as means to ends. This is what I take Kant to have meant by his injunction, "Treat humanity, whether in yourself or others, always as an end and not simply as a means."

Not every aggregation of interacting persons deserves the designation "community." When buyers and sellers, employers and workers, encounter one another in the market place, for example, each man treats the others as means to his own ends. To the salesman, the customer is an opportunity or an impediment, but not a person. The progressive transformation of human relationships into instrumental transactions is the feature of industrial society most severely criticized by both radical and conservative social philosophers.

A community of *learning* differs from all other kinds of community, such as a political community, a religious community, a community of work, or an artistic community, in the character of its collective goals and the forms of activity and organization which flow therefrom. The university is a community devoted to the preservation and advancement of knowledge, to the pursuit of truth, and to the development and enjoyment of man's intellectual powers. Furthermore, it is devoted to the pursuit of these goals collectively, not merely individually. The public discourse of the university community is not a mere *means* to the private activity of research, as John Stuart Mill seems to have thought. Rather, that discourse is itself one of the chief goods to be found in a flourishing university. It is precisely this devotion to an essentially collective activity that makes the university a community rather than an aggregation of individuals.

Certain obligations flow from the commitment to the values and collective enterprise of the university. Some of them, to be sure, are only fitfully honored in existing universities and colleges, but to a remarkable degree students and professors fulfill communal duties of which they are sometimes only dimly aware.

First in importance is the duty to treat truth as an end, as a good in itself, and hence never deliberately to utter falsehoods for ulterior purposes of whatever importance. The scholar must never misrepresent his research, falsify his data, doctor his sources, either for his own personal aggrandizement or in order to advance a theory whose validity he may devoutly wish to believe. If the facts show that intelligence is racially linked, or that the United States has been the aggressor as well as the defender—or indeed that she has *not* been the aggressor—then those facts must be stated openly and honestly. If the time comes when truth is superseded by some other good—if a lie can prevent a devastating war, or avert social chaos—then the community of the university is at an end. Those who would use the university as an instrument of political propaganda must answer for its death as a community of learning. I can imagine conditions under which I would be prepared to sacrifice the university to a higher good, but nothing resembling such conditions exists now in the United States.

From the primacy of the value of truth, and the commitment to a *community* of learning, it follows immediately that there is no place in the university for conflicting commitments which obstruct the search for, and expression of, truth. Secret research, for example, is inimical to the community of a university. Like a lie, the commitment to secrecy sunders the moral bond between the members of the university. A man who swears himself to silence on the results of his research is no more capable of entering genuinely into the public discourse of the university than is an FBI agent posing as a radical student.*

Quite obviously, on this interpretation of the ideal of the university, the phrase "Catholic university" is a strict contradiction in terms. A man may be ever so devout and still be a genuine member of the community of learning, so long as he makes himself the final authority of what he believes and confesses. But any man who binds himself to the doctrines enunciated by others, *whatever those doctrines may be and whether he perceives their truth for himself or not*—such a man is not an appropriate candidate for membership in the community of a university. Such obedience to dogma may be right, but nothing is gained by pre-

---

* On the same grounds, we must insist that our ideal university is no place for an *agent* of any religious or political movement. A dedicated believer in the American version of the cold war myth is welcome, but not an *agent* of the CIA. A devotee of things Russian or Chinese, but not an agent of a communist *or any other* party, foreign or domestic. What matters is not the character of the belief, but rather the autonomy of the believer. Agents of parties, representatives of dogmas, are welcome as visitors to the university, but in order to join our community of learning a man or woman must be unencumbered by conflicting moral commitments.

tending that it is compatible with the moral obligations of the community of learning.

Beyond the primary commitment to truth and the subsidiary obligations which flow from it, lie other obligations which bind together the students and teachers of a university. A professor is morally bound to present his subject matter honestly, to prepare himself adequately, to exhibit patience with students who are slow to learn. He has an obligation not to misuse his classroom authority, for example, by turning aside with ridicule a question he cannot answer, or by attempting to persuade students of his own beliefs with meretricious arguments. Students have an obligation to prepare themselves for class, to attend to their classmates as well as to the professor, to press objections and raise questions, in short to participate in the public discourse of the university as active members of the community.

If these injunctions seem banal or trivial—if they seem not to constitute a catalog of *significant* obligations—try for a moment to imagine a university in which they were systematically violated. Imagine a university in which the *typical* professor lectured as little as he could, ignored classroom questions, handed out grades at random, made no comments on students' papers, never met with colleagues or students, and put out even minimal effort only when a dean was looking over his shoulder. Imagine too a university in which students cheated at every turn, literally cared only for the grade and the degree, gave no time or energy to extracurricular activities, and felt no twinge of embarrassment at holding confused or unsupported opinions. There may be institutions in America which answer to this dismal description, but no decent college or university even remotely resembles it.

A genuine community of learning is possible among men and women who are willing to pursue the common goals of truth, rational discourse, and the preservation and transmission of learning. This willingness, however, is not by itself a *sufficient* condition for the creation of such a community. The reciprocal obligations which bind the members of the community to one another can come into existence only through a social contract, either explicit or implicit.

I imagine the social contract of the university to read something like the following, with due allowance for variations reflecting the particular circumstances of the contracting parties:

The Social Contract of the Ideal University

1. We assert the fundamental purpose of this community to be the preservation and advancement of learning and the pursuit of truth in an atmosphere of freedom and mutual respect, in which the intellectual freedoms of teaching, expression, research, and debate are guaranteed absolutely.

2. We commit ourselves, each to all, to recognize the right of each member of the community to participate in the establishment and administration of our internal rules of conduct. Each of us pledges himself to respond to the interests, opinions, and grievances of the others; each of us acknowledges his continuing obligation to arrive at mutually acceptable principles of internal governance through open discussion and collective decision.

3. Recognizing that there may be differences among us on all matters political and social, extending even to the question of how precisely decisions should be taken within the university, we nevertheless pledge ourselves to work out collectively accepted rules of procedure, guided by our unconditional and unanimous commitment to the principles expressed in the first clause of this contract. Each of us promises to put that commitment above his convictions about particular matters of internal governance, *so long as he is genuinely persuaded that every other member of the community is bound by the same overriding commitment.*

4. Finally, on the understanding that every member of this community commits himself to the foregoing, we all pledge our support to whatever measures must be taken to defend the integrity of the community against attacks either from within or from without.

The key to the viability even in theory of such a contractual community is of course the first clause—the unanimous agreement on the purposes of the university community. On that unanimity of purpose rests the willingness of the members to overcome even very deep disagreements about the particularities of university governance. When men pursue diverse and conflicting goals, they invest the procedures for resolving their disagreements with great importance, for they quite reasonably fear that their vital interests are threatened by any arrangement which gives others power over them. But such matters loom much less large when there is general confidence in the mutual agreement on ends.

As an example, consider the aggravating issue of "student power," and particularly the demand that each member of the university be given one vote in the process of decision, no matter what his status. I don't myself believe that strict democracy is the most appropriate rule for the conduct of university business; the general commitment to intellectual excellence seems to call for a distribution of authority in rough conformity with demonstrated competence. But if I believed that every student and professor in my university genuinely shared my dedication to the values described in the first clause of the contract, I would be content to accept rules of governance which vested a voting majority in the student body. Indeed, it is just such a belief which reconciles me now to the collective authority of my department, even though I bitterly disagree with some of its members about the most fundamental points of interpretation of those values.

To our question, How should a university be governed? the utopian answer is: If the university is a true community of learning, bound together by a solemn contract like that proposed above, then any system of university government is acceptable which serves the collective purposes of the community and arises from a collective agreement of the sort indicated in clause three. In such a community, the rules of order are mere instruments of convenience; they raise no fundamental questions, and the less attention paid to them the better.

One final word about the fourth clause of the contract. We are so accustomed to the injustices, repressions, and hypocrisies of contemporary society that we tend automatically to extend the greatest possible latitude to those who go beyond dispute or dissent to outright violations of law. A young man in America today obviously has a moral right to refuse to fight in Vietnam, even if he must lie, cheat, or flee the country to evade punishment. He is no more free than was my great-grandfather, who fled from Russia in order to avoid serving in the Czar's army. Eventually, we come to suppose that any sort of disruptive or illegal behavior is sanctified by the dictates of subjective conviction, so that we have a bad conscience about defending ourselves against attacks however outrageous.

This diffidence is probably appropriate as a rule of thumb, but there is no place for it in our utopian community of learning. So long as the founding contract is honored by the entire community, the members are perfectly justified in protecting their university, *even if the only effective means is the police power of the state.* Professors who conduct secret research, students who seek to use the university as an instrument for extraneous political purposes, administrators who serve corporate or governmental interests, have no place in our university, and the entire community should unite to throw them out.

But all of this is hopelessly utopian. Taking things as they might conceivably be, rather than as they ideally ought to be, how should a modern American university be governed?

2. ALL POWER TO THE FACULTY AND STUDENTS

The fundamental principle of governance in American colleges and universities today must be All Power to the Faculty and Students. It may well be that university progress, as commonly conceived, requires strong presidential leadership of the Hutchins or Conant variety. But the changes that really need to be made in our institutions of higher education simply will never issue from the sorts of men who would be acceptable to present-day boards of trustees and regents. We are in an age not of giants but of crisis managers—men skilled at keeping the lid on, adjusting to the rapid flow of pressures and counterpressures. Such men conceive of progress in all the wrong ways—as sheer growth, or as technological development, or as an even more intimate involvement with the federal government.

We must set ourselves *three* goals in the sphere of university governance, each more difficult than its predecessor. First, we must seek to block those particular decisions which corrupt and demean the university. I have in mind the decision by a president or board of trustees to lend the resources of the university to criminal acts of foreign aggression, as at Michigan State University, or to permit the cordoning off of buildings and corridors for secret research, as at MIT.

Second, we must seek to bring the process of decision into the open so that it can be subjected to criticism, to review, and ultimately to control by the university community. In particular, budgetary decisions affecting endowment and operating expenses must be called forth from the dark recesses in which they now hide. At Columbia University, to cite one particularly shocking example, the Treasurer reports directly to select members of the Board of Trustees, bypassing even the President. It is literally impossible, save by court order, for even blue-ribbon committees of senior Business School professors to obtain an accurate and detailed list of Columbia's real estate holdings. Major decisions have been made without review or accountability for thirty years now. This sort of administrative dictatorship must be ended.

Finally, we must strive whenever possible to adopt decisory procedures which encourage the natural growth of a university community. Despite the present impossibility of instituting a genuine rational community based upon a social contract, as outlined above, it is nevertheless perfectly possible to select modes of internal governance which foster rather than stifle communal ties. In particular, we must shun the multiversitarian tendencies which Dr. Kerr so blithely recounts, for the pluralist politics which emerges in the multiversity sets interest group against interest group in a manner totally destructive of genuine community.

Within a university run by faculty and students, the precise division of authority must be adjusted to the particularities of the situation. I can see no universal a priori principle which could command our allegiance in every possible situation. Nevertheless, some general rules can be suggested as plausible guidelines in today's universities.

First of all, let us repeat that the living arrangements of undergraduate men and women should be determined by the students themselves, subject only to such constraints as are imposed by the need for maintaining the condition of the dormitories and meeting costs. By and large, this is no longer a live issue among university administrators. So long as they can appear to be giving in to irresistible student pressure (so that parental and alumni protests can be deflected), college deans are quite happy to be rid of the dispute.

Curricular matters should be decided by joint committees of faculty and students, with maximum flexibility of curricular changes in response to genuine student interest. There is no point in trying to teach something to a student who doesn't want to learn it, and if a teacher cannot arouse his students' interest in the subject which he himself considers important, he probably won't accomplish anything by forcing it down their throats. What should the balance be? Here I can offer no hard and fast rules. But let me repeat one word of caution: if faculty and students feel themselves to be so totally at odds that neither is willing to grant the other a bare majority in a decision-making committee, then we can be quite sure that no arrangement will make genuine education possible between them. One might as well call in a labor arbitrator to settle a dispute between the first and second violin of a string quartet. Even if justice were done, beauty would scarcely be served.

Obviously, our faculty-student university will obey the familiar rule that no person should sit in judgment on himself. Students will not grade their own examinations; professors will not take part in the deliberations concerning their own promotion or tenure. But should students share in the promotion and hiring authority? Because of the virtual irrevocability of tenure decisions in

American universities, this is the touchiest question in the entire structure of university government.

At this point, feeling and reason pull me in opposite directions. Reason tells me that every argument which I have advanced thus far in support of some measure of student power applies with equal force in the present case. If students are to vote on curriculum, on discipline, on the selection of deans, even on the disposition of the endowment, why not also on hiring, promotion, and tenure? And yet, my soul cries out, "Here I draw the line!" Let me confess that I would prefer the decisions concerning hiring and promotion to be made by the faculty alone. My reasons are all perfectly sound: students lack experience and technical knowledge of the field, they are too easily swayed by classroom pyrotechnics of dubious educational value, they cannot measure a candidate's merits against other men and women in the field. And yet, I have watched great philosophy departments issue, after solemn deliberation, some of the godawfulest wrong decisions anyone could imagine. Would justice and utility really be better served by excluding students from this area of decision? I don't suppose they would.

So let us say that I endorse the principle of student participation in *all* academic decisions save their own certification, albeit grudgingly and with privately mumbled reservations.

One question remains: how can the faculty and students take decisory authority away from administrators, trustees, and boards of regents and vest it in themselves, where it belongs? The answer is simple and really quite traditional, though difficult indeed to put into practice: *Solidarity!* If the entire body of professors and students will stand together on this single issue, there is not a dean, president, trustee, or regent who can stand against them. Let the professors and students meet in a body (near a tennis court, if one is handy) and declare that henceforth they will be governed only by men of their own choosing and laws of their own enacting. Let such a step be taken first at a great Ivy League university, then at elite private colleges, finally at the great state universities. I have no doubt that such a movement would sweep all before it and usher in a new era of university governance in America.

A tempting vision came to me in the Spring of 1968 at Columbia, where a troglodytic Board of Trustees resisted the broadly based demand that charges be dropped against those arrested in the two police actions. Suppose that the President and Trustees had expelled a student whom the university—that is, the faculty and students—wished to retain. Very well, we could have said. *You* have expelled this undergraduate. *We* declare that he is still enrolled. *We* shall continue to instruct and examine him; *you* may admit a replacement, whom we will neither instruct nor examine. At the appropriate time, *we* shall present our student with a diploma bearing the signatures of the entire faculty and student body, testifying that he has completed our requirements for the bachelor's degree. *You* may present *your* candidate with a diploma bearing the official Columbia seal, signifying merely that the Board of Trustees has conferred a degree upon him. Then let us see which "graduate" is admitted to medical school or law school or graduate school; let us see, in short, whether the rest of the academic world considers *our* man or *yours* to be a true Columbia graduate. Can anyone doubt the outcome? An unofficial piece of paper bearing the signatures of Ernest Nagel, Lionel Trilling, Meyer Schapiro, and all the other distinguished members of the Columbia faculty is worth ten thousand official diplomas backed by nothing but a collection of administrators and trustees.

Carry this agreeable fantasy one step further. Suppose that the trustees were to stop payment on all salary or scholarship checks and were to fire the entire faculty and student body. They would then be the legal possessors of an enormous physical plant and a four hundred million–dollar endowment, but would they be a university? If the faculty and students sued for a release of funds, on the simple grounds that *they* are the university, and hence have a right to its endowment, how would the courts decide? What a grand case *that* would be!

But enough of these Clifford Odets scenarios! Somehow or other, in the decade to come, there is more to be gained from a university senate than from a general strike. One way or another, professors and students must recognize their common interest and unite in an attempt to take effective control of the major decisions in the university.*

* Since these words were written, we have witnessed the magnificent spectacle of ten thousand Harvard students and faculty massing in the Harvard stadium to decide collectively the course of their strike. At Cornell, six thousand students held an all-night vigil which turned the faculty around. There may be some timid observers who cannot tell the difference between democratic participation and mob rule, but I for one consider these great convocations to be the most encouraging events in the American academy in some time.

Practical Proposals for Utopian Reform

The time has come to pull together the strands of my argument and offer specific proposals for the reform of higher education in America. In the course of my discussion, I have criticized a number of features of the contemporary college and university scene. Some, like the use of the university to sort candidates for scarce and desirable slots in the economy, are rooted so deeply in the organization of American society that they could only be eliminated in the course of a thoroughgoing social transformation. Others, like the ambiguities and confusion of the Doctor of Philosophy degree, can perfectly well be rectified within the present framework of American society and education. In describing my proposals as "practical," I mean to indicate that they all fall far short of a revolution, either in education or in the economic and political organization of our society. They are "utopian" in the sense that they derive from a vision of the good society and the ideal university toward which I would like to see us move.

In order to introduce some system into these recommendations, let us begin with the point at which a student enters the world of higher education and then proceed stage by stage through the successive levels at which reforms might be called for. There are four distinct stages on which I wish to focus attention—namely: the transition from secondary school to college; the undergraduate experience; the sorting out of college graduates into professional or graduate programs; and the two, three, four, or more years devoted to professional training and certification.

We are all familiar with the pattern which prevails throughout American education today. The high school senior, usually sixteen or seventeen years old, applies early in the Fall to a number of colleges for admission the following September. After a procedure which varies from *pro forma* examination of his credentials (in a number of city and state colleges) to a rigorous competition for extremely scarce places, the young man or woman undertakes a four-year, full-time undergraduate program of courses leading to a first, or bachelor's, degree. On the basis of his performance, which is graded at every step along the way, he is more or less eligible for an array of attractive graduate fellowships, assistantships, and traveling grants after graduation. Another admissions squeeze, this one more severe than the first, sorts the college seniors into law schools, medical schools, graduate schools, and so on. And finally, the graduate grind, leading in almost every case to certification, a higher degree, and a career which will carry the student somewhere into the middle or upper-middle class of American society.

In my opinion, every single stage of this decade-long process needs thoroughgoing revision. The rationale for the changes I shall propose can be found in the first three Parts of this book; but beyond recommending particular changes, I should like to see the overall shape of higher education altered, so that a young man or woman nearing the end of secondray schooling confronts a fundamentally different educational system at the college or graduate level.

Let us begin with the aspect of university education which the adolescent first encounters: the college admissions system. In the third chapter of Part Two, I analyzed the destructive impact on high school students of the competitive admissions system which has grown up in the last quarter century. I argued there that the evil consequences of the admissions rat race flowed directly from the nature of the competitive situation, and not from any remediable unfairness or inefficiency on the part of the college admissions officers. Indeed, the worst pressures on aspiring high school seniors were seen to grow out of the very dedication of the elite colleges to an absolute even-handed justice in their criteria of admissions.

The root of the trouble is of course the fact that there is a genuine objective difference between the best colleges and those which are merely good or acceptable. The best colleges offer educational opportunities—on *any* theory of education—which simply cannot be matched at the general run of schools. What is more, the top colleges are in turn gateways to the best graduate and professional schools, from which it is an easy step to the preferred positions in the American economic and social hierarchy. In the light of these well-known facts, it is perfectly natural for high school students to aspire to the select colleges, and quite understandable that parents should goad their children to the exquisite performances required for admission. There is no point in mounting a nationwide advertisement campaign to persuade ghetto youth that a good job requires a good education, only then to condemn those middle-class parents who have learned that a great job requires a great education!

As I indicated at the end of my analysis in Part Three, there are only four ways in which the destructive pressure can be lifted from high school applicants, assuming that we cannot somehow deprive them of their natural desire for wealth, ease, comfort, status, approval, and exciting work. We can: (1) make performance in professional school irrelevant to one's social and economic reward; (2) make performance in college irrelevant to one's admission to professional school; (3) equalize the education offered in colleges, so that no school is very much to be desired over any other; or (4) divorce college admission from high school performance, so that the desirable places go neither to the able nor to the accomplished, but merely to the lucky.

The first alternative is, in terms of the limits laid down at the beginning of this chapter, totally *im*practical. It is already utopian to imagine a thoroughgoing reform of higher education; any proposal which also requires the complete transformation of the system of social rewards and distribution of wealth in America is clearly the other side of Utopia. Karl Marx's great principle of communist society—"From each according to his ability, to each according to his need"—carries us beyond the limits of *practical* proposals for reform.*

The *third* alternative, to equalize the quality of education now available in colleges across the country, also is ruled out on grounds of impracticality. To accomplish such an equalization, enormous amounts of money would have to be reallocated, and the faculties

---

* Of course, if "practical" is interpreted to mean "rational" or "humane" or "suitable for a good society," then no principle could be *more* "practical," but that is another matter entirely.

of two thousand colleges would have to be thoroughly shuffled. Something like this equalization does take place in state and city systems of public higher education, but so long as the upper levels of the academic pyramid are dominated by private institutions, no real homogenization will be possible.*

We are left with the second and fourth alternatives: somehow, performance in high school must be made irrelevant to college admission and college performance must be made irrelevant to graduate and professional admission. Let us begin with college admission.

The obvious solution to the problem, as I indicated in my earlier discussion, is a system of random distribution or admission by lot. Set some national minimal standards, and then assign places in freshman classes around the country to all those high school seniors who meet the standard. When I first published the analysis that appears here as the third chapter of Part Two, this proposal was greeted with derision by many of my friends and colleagues, including even the most radical among them. We are so imbued in America with the ethic of achievement that it seems positively criminal to deprive the front-running high school seniors of the fruits of their exertion. And yet, let us reflect for a moment on the arguments for my peculiar plan.

First of all, no high school student can reasonably be said to have a *right* to admission under any one system of admissions rather than another. He does of course have a right to fair treatment under whatever system is adopted, but larger consideration of social welfare must dictate *which* system is used to assign candidates to colleges. Various systems or principles might be chosen— for example, assignment by achievement (in which case some fair standard of measurement must be found); or assignment by ability (which is not at all the same thing as achievement); or assignment by achievement relative to ability (which corrects for genetic dif-

---

* As I have several times remarked, the advantages of heterogeneity, independence, and decentralization make it highly desirable that America *not* move in the direction of a monolithic state system of education. The only thing worse than the present high-pressure admissions process would be a uniform school system dominated by a state bureaucracy.

ferences, assuming they can be measured). Alternatively, one might assign candidates on the basis of the socially determined need for trained personnel, or with an eye to overcoming long-standing social inequities (as is now done through preferential treatment for Black students).

My principle differs from all of these. I wish to see students assigned to colleges so as to maximize the educational benefits which they derive from their schooling. Superficially, it might seem that this could best be accomplished by some principle based on a combination of achievement and ability. But, for all the reasons I have already given, the competition for scarce places at top colleges corrupts the secondary school education, and even corrodes primary education as well. Vital years in the lives of adolescent boys and girls are wasted in desperately cramming for college admissions. Countless teenagers sacrifice their youth on the altar of an Ivy League education.

The only solution is to sever the tie which binds high school performance to college admissions. I grant that a nationwide system cannot now be instituted, but here are some of the practical steps which could easily be taken to ease the worst of the pressures. Let the elite private colleges—the Ivy League, the Seven Sisters, the top men's schools—form an admissions consortium. Together, they can define some reasonable standard of minimum achievement and ability—a high minimum, to be sure, but one which is met by many more applicants than there are places. Each Spring, let them sort the applicants to all the schools in the consortium into two groups—"admit" and "reject." Then a computer can randomly select candidates from the "admit" category and assign them to colleges in accordance with their expressed schedule of preferences. Aspiring high school students will know that they need only rise above the minimum standard in order to be considered for admission. What is really important, however, *no improvement in their performance above the minimum will do anything to improve their chances*. The number-one student in the nation—accomplished pianist, creative physicist, published poet, political activist though he may be—will have exactly the same chance for admission to Harvard as the marginal man whose grades, college board scores, and other indices of achievement and ability just barely squeeze him into the initial "admit" category. All the pressure will be removed from students who clearly fall above the cutoff line because no possible benefit could come from an improvement in performance. A young man or woman could quite rationally calculate whether his record left room for some slacking off or experimentation.

Ivy League admissions officers will of course protest that any such system would bar them from considering the "intangible" factors on which they place such importance. No doubt. But that is a small price to pay for the nationwide sigh of relief that would go up from hundreds of thousands of anxious, overworked, parent-hounded boys and girls.

Once such an elite consortium had been established, other groups of schools could band together into similar "leagues." In some cases, the standards of these groups would merely be lower; in other cases, a group of colleges might decide to define criteria which were *different* from those of the Ivy bloc. Wherever applications signally outran places, the same system of random assignment would operate.

So much for my first practical proposal. It would not, by itself, revolutionize American higher education, but on a strict utilitarian calculus, it surely ranks among those social changes which would maximize happiness for the greatest number.

What shall we say of the undergraduate education which students encounter once they actually gain admission to college? It seems to me that undergraduate education is wrongly conceived and organized in almost every way. It begins too late, it lasts too long, it sets itself the wrong goals, and it pursues them in the wrong manner. Just about the only good thing to be said for undergraduate education today—and it is of course a great deal to say—is that somehow, under the worst of conditions, eager students do come into contact with dedicated, alert, provocative teachers. The result is real education, despite all of the harmful constraints and distortions that the college system can impose.

In the first place, college starts too late. For all sorts of reasons, young people today achieve at the age of fifteen or sixteen a level of social, sexual, and intellectual maturity which might possibly have been exhibited by eighteen- or nineteen-year-olds a generation ago. Countless high school students experience the same frustrating letdown in their senior year. It may be a useful time to cram for college-entrance examinations and plan the yearbook and prom, but emotionally, educationally, it is a waste. So let us eliminate the twelfth year of schooling and send students on to college (by random admissions, remember) at the age of sixteen or seventeen.

College itself ought to be totally divorced from preprofessional training. Students should be offered rigorous, challenging science courses, but no "pre-med" program; provocative social sciences, but nothing designed as "pre-law." There should be no undergraduate "majors" covertly designed to lock students into a doctoral track. The purpose of the undergraduate years should be intellectual exploration. However, there is a very peculiar misconception about exploration which pops up whenever proposals of this sort are made. Many staunch defenders of the educational *status quo* seem to think that exploration in the realm of ideas is like sampling at a smorgasbord buffet—a bite of this, a taste of that, but not very much of anything.

Nothing could be farther from the truth! Intellectual exploration is like the exploration of uncharted forests: in order to try it at all, one must commit oneself, plunge in, and keep going for long enough to discover whether there is anything to be found. A student who decides to explore sociology, let us say, must be free to bury himself in the subject, commit his whole mind to it, and follow it out for a month, a semester, a year, or longer.

But: he must *also* be free, at the end of his exploration, to return to his starting point, chalk the expedition up as a failure, and strike out in a new direction. Otherwise he loses the freedom which is essential to genuine exploration.

What does all this mean concretely for the curriculum and requirements of an undergraduate program? Clearly, it means a flexible program of offerings, including large lectures, small group discussions, directed study, and independent work, with no formal, rigid course distribution or degree requirements. Professors will be free to set difficult tasks and demand a high quality of work, but students will be free in their turn to drop out of one program and seek out another. In such a program, there is no place for grades, although as I have argued at some length, there *is* an essential role for rigorous criticism.

Not all students are alike in personality, intellect, tastes, and aspirations. Not all professors are alike in style of mind, modes of relating to students, or educational convictions. Obviously, therefore, no single form of undergraduate education will be universally suitable. There should be variation within institutions and among institutions. One college may be a small, rural community committed to intensive personal interaction and collective intellectual activity; a second may be a large, urban community, culturally heterogeneous, somewhat impersonal, devoted to privacy of the individual and idiosyncrasy of educational development. Under the ideal reconstruction of higher education which I am suggesting, students would be able to choose among alternative styles of undergraduate life, just as they do now. What is more, the absence of formal course credit and degree requirements would make transfers from school to school administratively easier, so that an eighteen-year-old would not be forced to persist in the choice he made when he was sixteen.

Let me say just a word more about my conception of undergraduate education in order to eliminate, if possible, one persistent misunderstanding. *Nothing I have said implies the adoption of a "permissive" or "indulgent" or "expressive" approach to education.* One of the consequences of our puritan heritage (which is notoriously shared by Jews and Catholics as well as Protestants) is the perverse and small-souled conviction that no one would ever do a lick of honest work if he were not either threatened or bribed into it. This mean-spirited view manifests itself in the pious horror of welfare "handouts" and the oft-expressed notion that under socialism everyone would goldbrick. It also manifests itself in the fearful prediction that a school without grades or rigid requirements would rapidly degenerate into intellectual finger painting and mud-pie making.

Now simple observation shows that this opinion of humanity,

realistically cynical though it is, just does not fit the facts. The laziest, most work-resistant people I have ever observed were the regular army sergeants in the units to which I was assigned during my brief, involuntary stint in the Armed Forces. The more authoritarian the institution became, the more devious were the attempts to circumvent its commands. By contrast, the hardest workers I know are Wall Street lawyers, successful businessmen, and tenured professors, all of whom would be quite free to goof off if they wished. What drives a seventy-year-old classicist to complete his twelfth book on the ancient Greeks is not rules, or degree requirements, or even economic reward and status, but simply a total emotional commitment to the project which he has freely chosen. When nonacademics voice the suspicion that junior professors publish only to secure tenure, they merely exhibit their complete ignorance of the academic world. Most productive scholars only get into their stride *after* they have been promoted to permanent positions; the change in status has little effect on their work, save to liberate their energies for even greater efforts.

Precisely the same generalizations are true of students (who are, after all, the lawyers, businessmen, and professors of tomorrow). The less rigid the regulations surrounding an academic program, the harder and more productively students work. There is of course no direct causal connection. The absence of rules does not stimulate fruitful endeavor any more than their presence does. The point is that students will pour their energies and intellects into their studies *only* if they are confronted by good teachers honestly presenting interesting material. Rules and requirements play a role when they *interfere* with genuine education by diverting the student's attention from the material which really interests him.

And after all, why should these facts surprise us? If I tell you that two dozen students have spent six weeks of their time memorizing lines, building scenery, rehearsing, and doing all the other tedious things that a theatrical production requires, *and all for the sheer enjoyment of it,* without promise of academic credit or financial reward, will you doubt my word on the grounds that no one would be willing to work so hard for "nothing"? Of course not! Such outpourings of energy are a commonplace of every high school and college in the country. And yet, if I suggest that those same students might be willing to slog through a text, do research in a library, and sweat it out in front of a typewriter, merely in order to have the pleasure of writing something subtle and meaningful about a Shakespearean tragedy or a philosophical argument, you will most likely dismiss me as a misty-eyed romantic with no appreciation of the real facts of human nature!

Well, my experience tells me that the cynics are wrong in this case. If you run a university like an army, then of course your students will act like soldiers on a pass whenever you let up on them for a moment. But if you run a university like a *school*, then you will get the same enthusiastic response to chemistry or philosophy or history that you now get to sports or amateur theatricals. Is there anyone who *really* doubts that Karl Marx, Feodor Dostoyevsky, Max Weber, Plato, and Shakespeare can hold their own against basketball and beer as campus attractions? With the sole exception of sex, whose lure I freely grant first place in the hearts and bodies of my students, there is not a single "extracurricular" campus activity which can beat the appeal of a free and honest interplay of ideas.

So let us not hear gloomy predictions of wicked sloth on our ungraded campus. The problem, as we discovered at Columbia, is not to get students talking about real issues once classes are canceled, but rather to get them to stop!

One problem is immediately apparent: all our utopian schemes for an ungraded, exploratory, educationally rewarding undergraduate curriculum are going to come to nothing, unless we can figure out some way to divorce graduate and professional admissions from undergraduate performance. We have already seen that high school education is corrupted by the pressures of college admission; in just the same way, college education is warped by the pressures of graduate admissions. Grades, requirements, and diplomas do not serve any purpose intrinsic to undergraduate education. Their role is to sort students into law schools, medical schools, doctoral programs, and so forth.

There are actually two distinct problems involved in the college-postgraduate transition. The first is the problem of sorting—that is to say, the ranking of candidates for scarce places in the most sought-after law schools, medical schools, or graduate programs. So long as the larger society offers greater rewards to the Yale Law graduate than to the NYU graduate; so long as a Berkeley degree in physics really counts for more in the world than a degree from Tennessee or Brown; then there will be an admissions crunch at the graduate level, and some sorting device must be found. The second problem is the need for preprofessional preparation. The science courses prerequisite to medical school, the mathematics needed for engineering, the languages demanded by classics or area studies, are all studied at the undergraduate level under our present system. If a high school senior thinks he might want to become a doctor, then he must fit math and science into his program in order to have any chance at all of admission to a medical school. But this directly interferes with the exploratory openness which I have been proposing for the college years. How can we preserve the independence of undergraduate education in the face of these pressures from graduate and professional schools?

Any solution must be a compromise, but I think there is a practical, workable solution which achieves much of the liberation I am arguing for. Let the undergraduate years be shortened from four to three, so that the typical student under our system completes his college education at the age of nineteen or twenty, rather than twenty-one or twenty-two. At this point, *any* graduating student who wishes to do so may take competitive, nationwide examinations for admission to graduate and professional schools. His college career, since it is ungraded and not standardized, will play no role in the graduate admissions procedure. Students who need special preparation for graduate programs will be offered the opportunity to spend a tough, concentrated fourth year taking courses specifically designed as preprofessional training for particular professions.

Obviously, many of the pressures which I have been criticizing will reenter the educational system at this point. I have already several times observed that these pressures cannot be entirely eliminated save by a total alteration of the entire American economy and society. But the cumulative effect of the reforms I have proposed is to put the pressures off to a point when students are emotionally and intellectually able to handle them. Instead of a constant, unremitting environment of anxiety, pressure, competition, and exhortation beginning virtually in kindergarten and persisting for sixteen years, we have a single high-pressure year which comes *after* the student has left college. Competition under this system becomes a temporary means to an end, not a permanent way of life.

Since successful completion of undergraduate requirements is *not* a prerequisite for professional or graduate training in my proposed system, there is obviously considerable flexibility for alternative career lines.

Ideally, I should like young men and women coming out of high school to have a choice between going to college and proceeding directly to professional training. There might occasionally be a student for whom three years of undergraduate education would be genuinely useless, a detour in a career already firmly chosen. But at the present time, such freedom would put intolerable economic pressure on many students to skip college and get on with professional school. One possible solution is simply to require every high school graduate to wait two or three years before entering preprofessional or professional training. It would be open to the student to spend the time in college (I am of course assuming that the United States is moving toward a system of guaranteed higher education for all), or at work, or in whatever other way he found fruitful and desirable. Young people with firm convictions about their careers could study their chosen field as undergraduates (but not for "credit"), or work at related jobs. It might be very useful for a seventeen-year-old future doctor to spend a year in a hospital as an orderly, getting a firsthand look at the medical world before making an irrevocable life commitment.

The central point is that the "undergraduate" years, either in school or out, should be devoted to the successful completion of a critical stage of intellectual maturation, *not* to the accumulation of precisely one hundred and twenty points of credit.

What sort of degree would the undergraduate in this new system receive? The obvious, if somewhat startling, answer is, *None*.

What could the degree signify, after all? That the holder of it had successfully completed the requirements for the degree? But there are no requirements. And since there are no grades, "successfully" has no meaning.

It is a trifle unsettling, I grant, to contemplate the idea of going to college merely for an education, rather than for a degree. But after one lives with the notion for a while, its strangeness somewhat recedes. Consider: what functions does the bachelor's degree play in our society? It sorts students for transmission to the next level of education; but we have made provision for that. It serves as a quasi-professional certification for purposes of hiring—a B.A. in physics or history testifies to *some* measure of employable competence. But under our system, the student who wishes such certification can perfectly well acquire it in the proper way, in a professional program *after* his undergraduate years are over.

The real function of the bachelor's degree in our society is certification, all right, but it is *class* certification, not professional certification. The B.A. stamps a man as a candidate in good standing for the middle class. It is the great social divider that distinguishes the working class from the middle class. Suppose there were no bachelor's degree. Suppose, that is to say, there were no official mark distinguishing those who went directly to work after high school from those who spent several years in college pursuing further study. What harm would be done thereby? Presumably, those who continued their studies would experience some benefit from it, though the difference might not be readily apparent. But corporations and government bureaucracies would be unable to demand the B.A. as a prerequisite for certain job categories. They would be forced to hire candidates on merit, and quite possibly some of the sharp class lines which now divide Americans would begin to blur.

There would still be men and women holding degrees, but they would all hold professional degrees directly related to their specific occupational competence. Since a bachelor's degree would no longer be prerequisite for admission to graduate programs, men and women past their early twenties could take the examinations and apply for admission. The rigid class-oriented career tracks could be broken down. At the present time, for example, an experienced surgical nurse cannot possibly go to medical school, even if she can find the money and is willing to devote four years or more to study. But under the system I am sketching, she could bone up for the competitive examinations and take them at the age of thirty or thirty-five. Her practical experience might very well help her to compete successfully against young candidates with superior educational advantages but no backlog of experience.

Thus, in countless ways, the rigid compartmentalization of American education could be somewhat dissolved. Quite obviously, the changes I have proposed, though hardly marginal, would still fall short of a total educational revolution. As I indicated at the outset of this chapter, my aim is to propose changes which could realistically be initiated within the present institutional framework. I am convinced that a great deal could be accomplished short of tearing the system down and building it anew from the base.

We come now to the last stage of the educational process: the professional and graduate schools themselves. I shall propose two reforms, both of which grow quite naturally out of what has already been said.

My first proposal is to sever the institutional connections between professional schools and their home universities. In my criticism of the model of the university as a training camp for the professions, I pointed to the conflicts of institutional loyalty which the medical school professor or teacher of law experiences. Professional schools are *essentially* certifying agencies. Their primary orientation is, and must be, toward the profession they serve, not toward the particular university with which they may be affiliated. It would be far better for the various professional schools to operate as independent institutions, even if none of the other reforms I have proposed were to be carried out. But quite obviously, if college is to be reorganized along the lines I have indicated, there is no reason why professional training programs should be sheltered under the same roof as undergraduate education.

The legal and economic complications of this proposal for cutting loose the professional schools are obviously very great. In some private universities, the professional schools have separate endowments, and the arrangements would not be impossibly difficult. In other cases, however, it might take a Solomon to determine precisely how the divorce should be carried out. At the very least, however, we can adopt the working principle that *new* professional schools or programs ought never to be introduced into the university, and the established schools should be separated wherever possible.

I have nothing to say about the internal organization and educational practices of professional schools in general. Since I have neither experience nor even secondhand knowledge of medical, legal, business, or engineering programs, I must pass over that sector of higher education in silence. I do have some experience of graduate education in the arts and sciences, however, and it has persuaded me that *very* great changes are desperately needed.

In my analysis of the peculiar character of the academic profession, I described the harmful contradictions which have developed in doctoral programs because of the attempt to combine professional training and certification with the nonprofessional initiation of young scholars into the activity of intellectual creation. As I pointed out, the doctorate is treated both as a certificate of competence in the professional role of college teacher and as a recognition of the successful completion of an original contribution to scholarship and knowledge. Since very few persons are genuinely capable of such a contribution, while many candidates desire and deserve professional certification, a species of systematic, collusive deception comes into existence. Time, energy, and enthusiasm are squandered on pseudotasks which accomplish nothing and fool no one.

The solution to the problem is obvious and eminently practical. What is more, this is the one area of reform in which broad pressures for change are already building up in the academic world, so that there seems to me to be a real chance for success here.

Very simply, let us abolish the degree of Doctor of Philosophy, and put in its place a three-year professional degree designed to certify candidates as competent to teach their subjects at the college or graduate level. The requirements for the degree should include intensive course work, independent study, some practice teaching under supervision, and perhaps even one or more lengthy pieces of written work. But *no* dissertation! No make-believe "original contributions to scholarship." Students should take the degree, as law and medical students do, in order to prepare themselves for a professional career, namely, college teaching.

Accompanying this strictly professional program should be a system of research grants for students who wish to engage in genuinely original research under the guidance of a senior professor. Students *could* apply for these grants immediately after completing their three-year training, but they would also be free to take teaching jobs and wait three or five or ten years before attempting original work.

Since there would be no degree higher than the teaching degree —no super–Ph.D., as it were—no one would be forced to write a lengthy dissertation merely to gain certification in the profession. Now, it goes without saying that the elite jobs would still be won by those young men and women who either did—or showed promise of doing—original research.* But the creative activities of scholarship would not become hopelessly and harmfully intertwined with the professional activities of training and certification. Stu-

---

* Strictly speaking, this statement should be amended to exclude women, for systematic discrimination in the higher reaches of the academic world excludes even the most brilliant women from the prestigious and attractive jobs. This fact is generally ignored by pious academic liberals, who bleed for Jews or Blacks while they refuse even to consider outstanding women for top jobs. Schools like Harvard, Princeton, Yale, and Columbia either will not hire more than a few token women, or else shunt them off into the corners of the institution. I am personally acquainted with a number of cases in which brilliant women at these institutions were denied regular tenured positions merely because of their sex. The vulgar locker-room jokes and smug sniggers which come to the lips of the noblest male professors when this subject is raised reveal them to be fixated at roughly the moral level of the Southern red-necked racist. Sometimes the source of the prejudice is homosexual hostility; sometimes it is the professors' infantile identification with the female candidate's children, for whom male chairmen of departments exhibit a quite remarkable and unprofessional solicitude ["Are you sure, Mrs. X, that your children will not suffer if you take this job?"]. But usually, the anti-feminism is just ordinary, garden-variety habit-encrusted prejudice.

dents who really felt no desire to write two or three hundred pages on a topic proposed by a professor would be relieved of that pointless task. Students who did wish to do original work would not be forced to squeeze it into the dissertation mold. And professors would be free to give honest, genuinely useful direction to apprentice scholars, because their intellectual judgments would not be distorted and constrained by considerations of a purely professional sort.

I have come to the end of my proposals for reform. Difficult as it will be to implement them, they quite obviously still fall short of the ideal. In particular, I have been forced to accept the practice of professional certification as an unavoidable fact of American society. My aim has been only to segregate the certifying procedure so that the secondary and undergraduate educational experiences are insulated from its pressures. So long as American society distributes wealth and status to the professionally successful, there is nothing to be gained from the fairy-tale pretense that competition can be avoided. But by making high school performance irrelevant to college admission, by making college performance irrelevant to graduate admission, and by removing professional training from the undergraduate curriculum, we can transform competition and certification from a way of life into a limited activity directly related to the student's self-interest.

One last word about the particular proposals which I have advanced in this final chapter. It may seem strange that, after a series of abstract analyses of ideal models and principles of governance, I should suddenly descend to the level of programmatic reform. Perhaps I can explain my motives, and at the same time pay homage to the teacher who most deeply influenced my own intellectual development, by concluding with a little story.

I had the great good fortune, during my senior year in college, to study with the famous Harvard philosopher Clarence Irving Lewis. Lewis, at the end of a long and distinguished career, was a very proper Victorian gentleman, complete with pince-nez. He was correct, polite, distant, and—to a young undergraduate like me—

terribly forbidding. I had studied a good deal of logic and analytic philosophy as an undergraduate, and I was well-supplied with an armory of sharp analytical tools with which to dissect any argument which crossed my path. Lewis required a term paper in his course on the theory of knowledge, and I elected to have a go at David Hume's copy theory of ideas. I slashed away at it for twenty pages or so, pretty well reducing it to stew meat, and Lewis made a few moderately complimentary remarks about my destructive arguments. Then, more as an afterthought than as a criticism, he wrote: "I should hope that the general character of this paper is not a symptom of that type of mind, in philosophy, which can find the objection to everything but advance the solution to nothing."

I hope that after finding objections to imperfections at every stage of higher education, I have at least advanced a solution for some of them.

Index